AF189728

Reaching Goals With Ease

Courageously Follow Your Own Path

Ulrike Bergmann

Bibliographic information of the German National Library:

The Deutsche Nationalbibliothek (German National Library) lists this publication in the Deutsche Nationalbibliografie; detailed bibliographical data can be found on the Internet at http://dnb.dnb.de.

Title of the German original:
Mit Leichtigkeit zum Ziel. Mutig dem eigenen Weg folgen.
© 2014 Verlag C. H. Beck oHG, München 2014

Production and Publishing:
BoD – Books on Demand, Norderstedt

ISBN: 978-3-7494-6973-4

Enjoy the journey on your personal path. There is no better path than the one you're on.

HOW TO USE THIS BOOK

The following elements will help you find your way around the book:

Tasks

Tasks and exercises support you in transferring the contents to your personal situation and gaining insights.

Examples

Examples and longer quotations from everyday life illustrate what has been said. They are put in boxes.

The memory boxes contain important aspects that you may ponder upon and keep in mind while working on your goals and projects.

Next Steps

At the end of each chapter you will find a recommendation on how to implement the content and what steps you can take next.

TABLE OF CONTENT

INTRODUCTION

Imagine you could have, do or be anything in the world. Do you know what that would be? Or does this concept feel out of reach for you? And would you accept what you wish?

Imagine furthermore that you would be given an approach that would make it easy for you to turn all your wishes into reality. A method that would be simple, because it suits your individual pace and your personal nature – and that shows you how to reach your goal with ease.

How does that feel? What triggers that idea in you? Are you willing to give up a few things for this to happen?

You may feel like one of my workshop participants. When I spoke to her about the theme of this book – how to get there with ease – her first reaction to it was indignation. She was fed up with all those promises that only sell books and convey concepts. This would fool people into believing something that is simply not possible.

Why am I telling you this? Because I know that it is possible to reach goals with ease and to achieve the results you want. The above-mentioned participant has also changed her mind in the meantime.

Ease is a State of Being

Ease is not for sale. You will not find it in any shop. Nor by reading this book. Ease arises when you change your attitude and posture and thus make other results possible – creating a different inner state from which you shape your everyday life.

> Ease is a choice – and demands a decision from you. It arises when you perceive what is happening and pay attention to what you think and how you act.

And something else is important:
Ease means something different for everyone.

A basic question runs through this book, which you may ask yourself again and again while reading: May it be easy for me? Your answers tell you where you hold beliefs that have been fed to you from an early age. For most of us, they have become so self-evident that we no longer question them. Such beliefs, which are worth reviewing, are reflected in sentences like this:

- Only what you've worked hard for has value.

- There is no such thing as a free lunch.

- You always take the easy way out (again / once more)!

You will recognize your basic patterns when you actively work with the exercises in this book and pay attention to your thoughts – especially the points where you react angrily, defensively or doubtfully. These reactions will give you clues as to where to start if you want to experience more ease – whether this be in terms of goals, the subject of this book, or in other ways.

From Heaviness to Ease

It is less the goals themselves that make it difficult for us, but rather what we have learned about goals – not only through our education, but above all through the cultural imprints with which we have grown up. These are unknown in other cultures, as I will show you in a moment.

Goals Require Decisions

If we have or want to achieve something new, we have to make room for it and decide what to let go of. In the German-speaking world, we speak of "hitting" or "cutting" a decision. What images do you see when you read this?

"Hitting" a decision is to "hit the mark". As if there were a target in front of us: a black circle in the middle, surrounded with colored circles. If you miss the center, this is an erroneous shot – or transferred to goals: a wrong decision! Missed! Insufficient!

It gets even more interesting when you "cut" a decision. What picture do you have of this?

In my workshops these are the two most frequent ones:

- *Cutting down a tree.* Once felled, the tree is doomed to death. You can't say, "I'm sorry, it was a mistake!" It's over and done with. Even if you put the two separate parts back together again, the tree will not grow together anymore.

- *Head off with the guillotine.* The result is somewhat more drastic, because this is not about a tree to which many people have little emotional access, but about a human body part. The result is the same in both cases: It can't be changed anymore.

No wonder that many people are afraid of choosing a goal or committing themselves to something. Targets have a weight with us, as if they were carved in stone. We are measured – or we measure ourselves – by the fact that we hit the mark right at the center.

But goals are alive and can change after a short time if we set off, gain experience and gain new insights. But what is carved in stone is difficult to change. In any case, traces remain that are recognizable to all.

Look at your associations with goals:

- What do you associate with goals?
- Is it easy for you to commit to something, or do you find it difficult?

Many people think that if they don't commit, they won't do anything wrong. But with this they give up the chance to shape their lives according to their own ideas. But in the end, all that matters is whether you're satisfied or not. No one else can live your life for you. Only you yourself are responsible for ensuring that one day – and especially in old age – you are satisfied with what you have achieved, experienced and shaped.

Other Languages, Easier Ways

A look at other language areas and cultures helps here. In English, decisions are made. This has something to do with craftsmanship and the ability to create something yourself. I experienced it the same way during my longer stays in the USA and Canada: the awareness of having control over my goals and being able to shape them is much more pronounced in both countries than it is in Germany.

I find the Romanic languages even more impressive. Let us take French as an example: *prendre une décision* – taking a decision. Here I see the picture of a large tub containing a wide variety of possibilities. From this I take the option that I like best. I look at it from all sides, try it out like a pair of shoes and finally decide if I feel comfortable with it, if it suits me and if I want to go with it.

If not, I put it back – and take another option. Ah, what a relief! That's life. It offers many possibilities, and only if you try some of them will you know which ones really suit you. You can choose and consciously decide for it.

Task: Fill the Tub

Imagine having a magic wand that gives you everything you have, do or want to be. Use it for the area in which you are currently most longing for a change. Fill your water vat with everything you can imagine. Be brave and let your imagination run wild. Make a game of finding as many wishes as possible.

In this way, you will experience an abundance that is downright lavish. If you find it difficult to go with this idea, please

13

write down all the thoughts that go along with it. We need both – the abundance and the restrictions – again in other places.

Choose the Path of Least Resistance!

What if there were not one single or right way, but innumerable ways that lead to the goal? Just as there are hiking trails, side roads, main roads and motorways on which you can reach your destination – according to your wishes and time frame? These include those that are less strenuous because they fit you, your personality and your needs.

For this easier procedure, I have chosen an image: the river that meanders through the landscape on the path of least resistance. It gently flows around obstacles or sometimes takes smaller chunks with it for a while until it releases them again.

Perhaps situations come to mind when you heard a sentence that was seldom meant as a compliment: you make it easy for yourself and once again choose the path of least resistance. In it the reproach resonates that we make it too easy for ourselves, shy away from arguments and avoid conflicts. It's time to let go of that link and seriously look at what is really in that picture.

For goals, the path of least resistance is the best way to get results easily. Take water as your role model. It flows and finds its way where it's easy. It moves around obstacles, even if this means a change of direction. What can develop from this over time can be seen in natural wonders such as the Niagara Falls or the Grand Canyon.

The path of least resistance is easy, but not always simple. Here, too, you have to act and do something about it – but at a different speed. Sometimes you move ahead slowly and splashing; then the speed changes again and you flow freely and briskly towards your goal. Sometimes a detour is necessary because obstacles make it difficult to get ahead. But as the saying goes: detours expand your knowledge of surroundings. In this way you will discover better and better how it is easy for you. You'll see where courage is needed to break new ground and how to make your journey enjoyable.

Preparation for Our Journey

Have you got the desire to go on a journey with me? Here are the most important aids for your path: for your notes and idea collections get yourself a nice notebook or a folder that you like, a small notebook or a pad for spontaneous ideas when you are on the road, colored felt-tip pens or a special fountain pen with which you like to write.

CHOOSE WHAT YOU WANT!

What do you feel when you read this headline? Is it anticipation or do you experience a feeling of insecurity? Maybe a mixture of both.

Changes as a Starting Point

Usually the starting point for goals is the desire to change something and to shape life differently. Therefore, we start with an inventory of your current situation and focus on what you want to achieve. Both belong together: where you currently stand and where you want to go. Only from this combination does the motivation arise to set oneself in motion and to take concrete steps.

Task: Identifying the Starting Point

- *Start by becoming aware of where you are. From there it is easier to determine the direction, route and destination. How satisfied are you in the most important areas of your life (activities, relationships, finances, health)? Use a scale from 1 (not at all) to 10 (everything is fine) for each area.*

- *In which areas is your dissatisfaction the greatest? What specifically bothers you? List all aspects that are different from what you want them to be.*

- *What has the highest priority? What do you want to change first? Put all the points in order according to their degree of importance.*

- *Make a note of any ideas and wishes you already have about each point.*

Collect your answers in your note book. In the next few weeks, write down any other ideas or things that you might want to address in some way. Flip through it again and again and let it inspire you.

Personal or Other People's Goals?

Goals should unfold in us so much enthusiasm that they fire up our actions again and again. Powerful goals fit our circumstances and are in harmony with what is important to us: in life, at work and in relationships with other people. Then they inspire us and carry us when obstacles or challenges arise, because we are prepared to stick to them and temporarily accept inconveniences.

Nevertheless, many people do not recognize their own goals at first and unconsciously adopt other people's goals. They pursue the dreams of others (parents, peers, superiors, colleagues, society, media), even if they do not correspond to them or if they have other ideas about a fulfilled life. After all, we all want to belong – a basic human need. This makes it difficult to strike a balance between one's own ideas and the demands or recommendations of others. Sometimes it takes some time until we find access to what we want ourselves.

> ### *Simon, Attorney at Law, Coaching Client*
>
> *After graduating from high school, Simon had no concrete idea of what he wanted to do for a living. What he knew was that he had a strong talent for languages. This was shown by the*

fact that besides German he could speak fluently Spanish as well as English and French. In the career counselling service at the employment office, he was recommended to study to be-come a teacher or to train as an interpreter and translator. He could not imagine either, and so a third option came into play: the combination with economy or law.

In his last school year, he had taken part in a legal work-group and therefore opted for law. He successfully completed his studies, albeit without much enthusiasm. After his bar exams, he worked in a law firm until he realized that he had followed external ideas with his studies: His mother would have liked to become a juvenile judge, but could not realize this wish. And the legal workgroup had above all served to be able to better stand up to his father in discussions.

After he had discovered this, he wanted to find out his true desires. The result was a solution in which we combined his career to date with his interests to create new opportunities. Today, he supports law firms in winning more clients through customer-oriented communication.

Check regularly whether your wishes and goals really meet your own expectations or whether you are fulfilling someone else's dream.

Bring Head and Heart into Harmony

As Simon's example shows, it is important to find out what wishes you have for your life. You alone decide how you want to shape your life and where the journey will take you. Your mind can give you clues that will help you understand what is important and what is right. It is from there that the critical voices come, which reject them as senseless or impossible.

These critical voices and doubts are hardly considered in the usual procedure for achieving goals. There you essentially follow the sequence "decide – plan – implement". This procedure requires a certain tunnel vision with which the target is kept firmly in view. Anything that doesn't fit will be hidden. There's little room for feelings.

However, this lacks one essential factor: what your heart says about it. When it comes to personal wishes and ideas for the future, it is the better advisor. In your heart sit your feelings, without which your ideas resemble bubbles that rise from time to time – and quickly burst again. Only when you listen to your heart do you recognize which of your wishes make something in you resonate. The question now is how good your access to this guide is. If its impulses have been ignored or fended off for years, it only makes itself noticed quietly. Then you will need some time until you can trust this voice again.

The Encouraging Principle, which you will get to know in the next chapter, supports you in reconnecting head and heart. This procedure is as individual as you are, based on your needs and adapted to your life situation. You use it at your own pace and in the way that suits you. Instead of leaving supremacy to your mind, which wants to regulate everything with reason, you involve your heart, pay attention to your feelings and follow these indications.

Recognizing What is Important and Right

Your inventory at the beginning of this chapter showed you in which area you have the strongest desire for change and what is your highest priority. You may also feel pressured to act quickly instead of waiting even longer. But do you already know the direction in which you want to move?

A lot of people have a hard time with it. They know what they don't want (anymore), but they lack ideas of what they want instead. Many therefore stay far too long in unpleasant or even sickening situations and hope that one day they will be struck by the lightning of knowledge. This may take a while …

How I Found My Calling

My path of change began with a surgery-related breakdown. During these seven weeks of absence from work I realized that I urgently needed to change my job. But what, I was unclear. I was with the best employer I could think of. The general conditions were fine – and yet I felt a dissatisfaction, which I could classify but not change.

So I waited and trusted that the right thing would show up at the right time. In the meantime, I reduced my daily working hours, returned to private interests and saved as much money as possible to ensure that I could do something completely different without financial pressure.

The waiting phase lasted 18 months. One day I was sitting in an internal seminar when suddenly the knowledge struck me like lightning: What the speaker did, that's what I wanted to do. I immediately thought of countless situations that encouraged me in this wish and showed me that it was the right way for me.

Another 18 months later I left the company, for which I had worked for almost 14 years. This was the beginning of my path to independence.

Waiting is not possible for everyone. And not necessary, too. In contrast to the late 1980s, today there are many good approaches that lead to the goal much faster. One of them is to deal intensively with one's own wishes and dreams and to connect more and more with them. This will enable you to recognize the potential they hold and how you to achieve lasting satisfaction.

Wishes and Dreams Show the Direction

Our daydreams as well as our repeated wishes often show us a possible future. However, many people do not take these clues very seriously. They dismiss their ideas as crazy, dream dancing or utopia. When they talk about it, they are usually additionally encouraged in this assessment by their environment.

Those who regularly ignore emerging wishes and ideas lead a life on the back burner. On the outside everything seems to be fine, but inside you know that something is missing and that you have expected more from life than a dream holiday or an adventure trip every now and then. After a few weeks these memories have faded and the grey everyday life again covers everything. At some point, travel and adventure are no longer enough to compensate for frustration and dissatisfaction. You feel empty inside, unhappy and far removed from what makes a fulfilled life.

Dr. Eva-Ellen Sieweke on the Subject of "Making Dreams Come True"

I grew up with the idea that I could be anything I wanted to be. Reality was different. I chose a course of study that hardly suited me, and my first job after that shocked me so much that I asked myself: Does work have to be so awful? How do the others do it? How can they take it?

This job tortured me and made me unimaginably unhappy. I finally quit it and kept on looking for the right job for two and a half years until I found it: Lecturer at the University of Düsseldorf and doctoral student.

Remark: After achieving her Doctorate in 2016 she found a position at the German Red Cross.

Deal with your wishes and dreams. Find out what inspires and fascinates you, which possibilities stimulate you and delight you.

Task: Recognizing Wishes and Dreams

If you still have no idea which direction you want to take, collect everything. Take your note book or a large sheet of paper. Write, paint or paste your answers to the following questions:

▪ *What have you always dreamed of?*
   Remember the ideas you had as a child. What the hell was that? What were you raving about? What did you want to be? Also ask in your environment what others still remember. Which of these still triggers positive feelings in you? Mark this in your collection.

- *Which activities fascinate you most?*
  Pay attention to which topics attract your attention and, above all, hold it – be it in books, in magazines, blogs or in television or radio reports. What keeps you busy for more than an hour, what has an effect or reappears later?

- *What are you losing yourself in?*
  Which tasks occupy you so much that you even forget to eat and drink?

- *What would you like to try?*
  Which occupations do intrigue you to such an extent that you get the desire to try it? Write down what's stopping you from trying.

- *Who do you admire or envy?*
  Admiration and envy show you what slumbers within you and is waiting to be noticed and seen. Details are also important here: Who is it? What's the person doing? What exactly fascinates you? Notice and describe the details.

Do this task for several days until you think you have gathered enough material. Write all the pints collected individually on sticky notes so that you can sort them according to different criteria. If something appears several times, write it as often as it occurs. This enables you to identify important, recurring factors more quickly. Find multiple criteria by which to sort. Be imaginative here and allow yourself to be creative and a little off-topic. It stimulates your power of combination. It is even better if you do this task together with someone who provides an additional view on it. Sorting criteria can be: alphabetical, by color or image, keywords, topics ...

Task: Analyze all Results

- *With these questions you analyze each result.*

- *What do the points have in common? What common theme do you recognize?*
  Examples: wordplay, international, innovations, courage to the unusual ...

- *Why does it appeal to you? What does this subject remind you of? What do you associate with this?*
  Examples: my enthusiasm for pop music; how I collected license plates on holiday; the competition with my brother in swimming; how easy it was for me to learn languages ...

- *Which of these do you want to follow up? What are you putting aside?*
  Possible selection criteria: The energy or vitality that you feel; the significance that the subject still holds for you today; the joy that is associated with it ...

Take a look at your collection. Does a topic particularly appeal to you – and perhaps make you a little afraid? Then you're on the right track. If this is not yet the case, do not fear. With the next steps you will find out what you really want.

What do You Really Want?

Now we're going even deeper into the realm of fantasy. That means you can be a little crazy. This awakens the creative side in you. And don't tell me you're not imaginative! Your imagination may not be particularly strong. But every human being has the ability to think something up. So are you.

You do it daily – when you think of all the negative things that could happen: that you're late, your presentation doesn't arrive, your child could have an accident on the way home... Usually all the horrible things we imagine don't happen at all. Your thoughts are pure fantasy. Even if these images or thoughts seem very real, they are nothing more than a result of your imagination. Use this gift to imagine the best you can think of.

Let Fantasy Rule, Think Big

Start by thinking as big as you can. Drop all barriers that have hindered you so far and allow yourself to be fanciful.

You already had an opportunity to do this in the introduction, when you were allowed to fill your tub. Did you do this? Then I'm sure you'll find it easy to get on with this task now. If not, now is the time to start.

Task: Expand Ideas Further

Extend your ideas of what you might have in your life far beyond what you have imagined so far. If you find it difficult to imagine this life for yourself, invent a fictional character to whom you give everything you can think of.

How about a person who has everything that seems possible – and much more. Where does s/he live? What's s/he doing? How does s/he spend his/her money? Who surrounds them?

Go one step further: What would be the craziest thing this person could experience?

Experience everything that makes up this life and feel what it feels like to have and be all this: proud, honorable, great, esteemed, powerful, sexy, admired, generous, powerful, humble, safe, free, alive, grateful ...

Take a bath in this imagination and let it wrap you. Stay connected to these feelings and write down what you experience and how it feels. That's all there is to it.

Do this task in a circle of friends or in a group of encouragers. Encourage each other to think bigger, crazier, wilder. If you allow yourself this fantasy, you will experience a surge of energy like seldom before. This stimulates your brain, which cannot distinguish between objective reality and what you create in your imagination. So, imagine the best thing you can dream of!

What if ...

The beginning of this sentence supports us in pursuing ideas and concepts and playing them through without immediately thinking about their implementation. It's just a mind game. However, one that can provide valuable insights. Years ago, when I thought about what it would be like to let go of a long-standing offer with this sentence, the answer was clear very quickly. I felt a great relief, which spread out in me as a feeling of expanse and freedom.

At this point, we will change the viewpoint and accept the following: All people have the desire to lead a content and happy life. No matter where they are at the moment and what still prevents them from moving forward. We're taking advantage of that now.

You have already learned a lot about yourself and your wishes on the basis of the previous tasks. In the meantime, you have also become more familiar with your fantasy. This will help you in the final exercise, which is about creating a vision of the future. This includes everything you desire in the four most important areas of your life: work, finances, relationships, health. So that you don't get caught up in thinking and evaluating, there is one condition associated with this: you have to write non-stop. Stay in touch with your feelings and write straight away.

Task: "I love my life."

Write at the beginning the following sentence: It is [month] [year plus 3] - and I love my life! [Month] stands for the current month in which you do this task, and [Year plus 3] for three years into the future. It will look that way: It's August 2022 - and I love my life! It offers me everything I have always wanted ... And now you describe what this includes. What if you love your life and it is exactly as you want it to be?

Write down everything you can think of for at least ten minutes without stopping. If you come to a standstill, write the sentence again: "I love my life!" This will re-connect you with the feeling of what it is like not to live with any compromises, but to be truly enthusiastic, happy and satisfied.

Notice again and again what it feels like to be alive on all levels. That's the only guideline for your description. Be courageous and describe what you imagine and want. No one but you will read or see these pages – unless you choose to share it with someone else.

The Vision of the Future Attracts the Result

With your description you anticipate your future. Every day read what you have written and expand your imagination. Make the details even more vivid. Add more elements. With it you bring your vision of the future into the present and make it come alive. This way, you connect again and again with everything you wish for and what makes you feel powerful and alive. You become a magnet, both for your goal and for an easy path to get there.

As already mentioned, our brain, which is connected to the subconscious, cannot distinguish between "imagined" and "real". It will therefore respond to your feelings and support you in attracting everything you need to create this reality. The better you stay connected to your vision of the future – especially on the emotional level – the more impulses you will receive for your next steps.

Meike, Designer, Participant in a Coaching Group, One Year After Her Participation

Now I understand why we should write this text at the beginning. At that time, I could not understand it and considered it an annoying exercise. But in the meantime, everything I wrote down at that time has actually happened.

Select a Project

The more detailed you have described your vision of the future, the more points it contains. I therefore recommend that you focus on one project for the next six months and give it your full attention. That doesn't mean leaving the others out of it. These remain anchored in you, develop there at their own pace and come to the surface at the right time. This happens automatically and without you having to do anything.

Think back to your initial situation: What did you want to change in the next twelve to 18 months? What is your top priority? This determines the selection of your project.

At the same time, I recommend that you choose a goal that meets the following criteria for working with the Encouragement Tools that I present to you in the next chapter:

▪ **Courageous** – You exceed your previous limits and expand your comfort zone. This refers to the area in which we can do and know everything, act routinely and are aware of our strengths, weaknesses and abilities.

▪ **Ambitious** – On the one hand, it challenges you to make a greater effort than you have done so far. On the other hand, you do not yet know how and whether it can be reached at all.

▪ **Desirable** - It's something you really want, and perhaps you've wanted it for a long time. But so far, fears, doubts or lack of support have kept you from achieving it. Decide now to give your goal more weight than all obstacles and uncertainties – so that it becomes a lived reality.

Which Project do you Choose?

Describe your project in a clear, complete sentence that contains a result – as if you had already achieved your goal. This means that there are no "softeners" such as "will, would, would like ..." contained in it. Use terms that convey feelings. Here is an example of a clear, emotional formulation of a goal: *I have found a field of activity that fulfils me and brings my abilities and experiences to bear.*

Firmly Anchoring Your goal

With the following suggestions you will keep an eye on your project and stimulate your subconscious to give you impulses again and again. Choose one or even better both variants:

▪ Give your goal an **attractive motto** or an **emotional name**. Such mottos can be: *Breakthrough to success ... Magnetism for my ideal customers ... Freedom that I mean! ... My year of love and happiness.* Or choose a short description like "Project Firebird" or simply a name like Laura, Egon or Rudi, with which you associate positive associations.

▪ Find a **symbol** that will remind you again and again of your plans as an optical anchor. Here are a few examples: a fountain for financial abundance, an eagle for freedom or ease ...

▪ Make your project visible in many places, e.g. as a photo on your desk, your mobile phone or as a background on your computer desktop. You can stick the name on your diary or your dreams notebook. The slogan can serve as a screen saver - if it moves there, it will be even more effective.

- If you are more of a haptic person, choose something easy to carry in your trouser, jacket or handbag, such as a soft toy, a shell or a stone, with which you associate positive memories.

Progressing in Small Steps

With large projects, it is easy to get a feeling of overwhelm when thinking about all the steps that are required. Focus on small steps that you can take every day, rather than thinking in milestones and big actions. A large number of small steps lead more easily to results than large chunks, which can only be implemented with a great deal of effort and strain.

These small steps are also called "work steps". These are the smallest possible units that you can complete within 15 minutes, e.g. make a phone call, read a book chapter, write a page of text ... Get used to doing at least one small step every day.

Act according to the motto: It is better to constantly take small steps, which can be taken along the way, than to take a big step every now and then, which costs a lot of energy.

Record your work steps in your diary or note book. This allows you to see at any time which route you have already travelled. If you find it difficult or lack the drive, look at how much you have already done and what results you have achieved. This will motivate you to continue with small steps.

Next Steps

- Select your most important project. Decide on a sub goal on which you are focusing first.

- Give your project a name or slogan, find a suitable symbol for it or create a collage with important details that remind you of your goal.

THE ENCOURAGING PRINCIPLE: THE EASY WAY TO SUCCESS!

With tools that fit your personality and match your individual way of working, it is much easier to reach your goal. This is the case with the elements of the Encouraging Principle. They offer an approach that allows you to discover the easiest way to reach your goal – but in a different way than usual. Instead of "how-to-instructions", which you use like a roadmap, the Encouragement Principle offers you a framework with which you can find *your* easiest way.

The Encouragement Principle connects all three levels of a person in the following way:

- On the **mental level**, you have already taken the first steps with the previous tasks. You have worked out what you really want and selected a project. There remains the question of whether you are fully committed and therefore ready to take all the necessary steps.

- On the **physical level**, you implement your ideas and get ever closer to your goal through committed action. Depending on your preference, you can set off alone or get support and encouragement from a support group or a coach. The more binding your actions, the faster and easier it is for you to reach your goal. You can also use your body as a compass for ease.

- These two levels are supported by the **spiritual dimension**. Here you connect with universal, collective energies. These show up as inner guidance, intuition or impulses to act. At this level, you get the right ideas for your next steps at the right moment. That can also sometimes mean waiting and doing nothing instead of acting just so that something is done.

In this chapter, you will learn about four Encouraging Tools that make it easier for you to move forward:

- **Decisiveness** – It paves the way to more ease.

- **Imagination** – A strong inner connection to your project acts as a magnet for coincidence.

- **Intention** – This allows you to anticipate the desired results and trust your inner guidance.

- **Commitment** – includes the willingness to implement emerging impulses without ifs or buts.

Decisiveness: Pave the Way

By determining your highest priority, you have determined the direction and decided which project to implement. But are you totally committed? We are often only half-hearted committed because we want to keep further possibilities open to us. However, this results in half-hearted results and the possible big success remains on the track.

Decisiveness Follows Decision

The selection was only the first step. Then came the decision for one of several possibilities. However, until you are really committed and determined to carry out your plan, you will keep all your back doors open: Maybe something else will come – a better opportunity, a more interesting project? It is only through your decisiveness that you do consciously stand by your choice. There is no "perhaps" any more, but only the "yes" to your project, which comes from the bottom of your heart.

With your "I choose it!" you underline your willingness to do all you can to achieve this goal – even if it is difficult, you have to break new ground or change habits. You stand by your goal – with no ifs or buts. Thus, your project receives your full attention and energy.

Axel Naglich, Austrian Extreme Mountaineer

The Austrian documentary film "Mount St. Elias" from 2009 shows in an impressive way how decisiveness can look like[1]. Before crossing a risky passage at an altitude of over 16,000 feet, extreme mountaineer Axel Naglich expressed it to his hesitant colleagues: "I didn't climb this far to give up now! "

Granted, this is an extreme example. Nevertheless, Axel Naglich can serve as a role model for your everyday life. Once you've made up your mind and committed to a goal, you'll experience how things can sometimes fit together in an almost miraculous way – even with smaller goals. The supposed "magic" arises from your determination to achieve your goal. Or as one American colleague puts it: *"It's not hocus-pocus, it's focus."*

Decisiveness and focus act like a magnet that attracts everything you need to achieve your goal at the right time.

---

[1] Official trailer of this film:
https://www.youtube.com/watch?v=_SBMeDlM-7Q

How Committed are You?

How can you tell if you're really committed? This question is frequently asked to me and is easy to answer: By the result of your actions. I would like to share an example of how decisiveness affects results.

From Two to Seven Participants

For a training of small business owners, which I had already successfully conducted several times, the registrations failed to materialize. On Sunday, three days before the starting date, only two people had registered. When I talked to a friend about it, she asked me the question: How committed are you regarding this training? Immediately I felt that the key was here: I was not decided!

On the one hand, I wanted the income associated with it, on the other hand, there were other topics that occupied me more. On the same evening I consciously decided to start the training with at least six people.

Where the participants were to come from was completely unclear to me at that time. But everything went well. On Monday I received a call which resulted in two registrations; on Tuesday another registration was received so that we started the seminar on Wednesday morning with these five people. After 20 minutes the door opened and a sixth participant appeared. For this one I had already provided a chair full of expectation.

The surprise was perfect when a seventh participant appeared after another half hour. He had decided to attend that very morning.

If things don't turn out as expected, I regularly ask myself the question: *How committed am I?* Sometimes I cancel an event because I know I don't want to commit at this point. Then what the US psychologist William James says applies: *"If you have to make a decision and you don't make it, that's a decision too."*[2]

With the power of decisiveness, you open the door to success. Use the following key question at every point of your path: *How committed am I (for my project / this (next) step ...)?*

Imagination: Anticipating Results

Putting a vision of the future on paper is the first step, which must now be followed by another: to keep reconnecting with the project and to present it in all its details. This is an essential point to reach your goal with ease. You visualize your goal and make it come alive in your imagination. You imagine all the details and anticipate the results. You already see yourself at your destination and feel what it is like to be there.

The more often you put yourself in your future world of life and work, the more details you add to your still blurred picture of the future. You create a clear, defined and vivid idea of what you want to achieve. This creates the previously mentioned focus, the inner orientation towards your goal, from which supposedly magical results arise.

---

[2] Quoted after Jochen Mai. Article "Wahlpflicht – Entschiedenheit ist mehr als zu entscheiden" ("Compulsory voting – decisiveness is more than just a decision") from 29.11.2009 in the Karrierebibel Blog, http://bit.ly/gRDAn2

How a High Attraction is Created

As long as you are concerned with your wishes, you remain in wanting. The only thing that is sure to come out of it is more wanting. There's nothing wrong with that. After all, many people want something to change in their lives and imagine what it might look like. Our wishes are the first step towards a change and therefore very important. They resemble a compass pointing in the direction of our interests, preferences and needs.

Unfortunately, the desires do not automatically come with ways and means to realize them. These only arise when you go beyond wishes and ideas into the mental state of having. To do this, you have to imagine that you already have, be, and do everything you want. Live already in your future. Let your dreams come to life. Your imagination will help you to do this. With it you build the bridge between the certainty of having and at the same time letting go of all wants. Sounds difficult at first, but with a little practice it will always get better. The prerequisite is that you understand that wanting and having are mutually exclusive. As long as you want something, you can't have it. Only when you are deeply immersed in all thoughts and actions in your idea of "having" does the path to it emerge.

On the one hand, this has to do with the fact that everything in the world, all inventions, achievements and procedures, are created twice: once in the imagination of one or more people and then brought into reality through focused actions. Before we can achieve a goal, there must be an inner picture of it. Only what we can imagine, we will realize.

Create Constructive Tension

Project yourself mentally into the future result you want to achieve. Supplement your imagination with all the details that are important to you and let them come alive with all your senses. As shown in this example:

Walking Around Your Future Home

You have the floor plan for your future home in front of you. Imagine walking through each room. With slow steps you measure the first room. You feel the soft carpet under your feet and experience the difference to the Italian terracotta tiles in the kitchen and entrance area. You see the new furniture that fits so well into the large living room with the floor-to-ceiling windows.

You open the patio door and step out into the spacious garden. As you slowly walk around, you experience the joy of looking at the variety of plants and the colorful blossoms. You listen to the birds that have built their nest in the trees. You smell the sweet scent of the flowers and pick some of the ripe currants. You feel how juicy they are and how the taste is spreading in your mouth. You remember the power you felt when you planted these bushes on the fence. You talk with your neighbor over the fence, who tells you how happy she is that you have moved into this house.

In short: you experience everything you want, already now with all your senses in your imagination. You can see, hear, smell, taste and feel every detail.

With your detailed vision of the future, a constructive tension arises through which implementation ideas and possible paths emerge. Your subconscious registers that there is a difference between the place where you are and your vision of the future. This deviation creates a tension that your subconscious dissolves by continuously giving you clues on how to overcome this discrepancy as quickly as possible.

Always bring this clear idea of your goal into your consciousness and keep it there – just as the captain of a ship directs his gaze to the port he is heading for. Meanwhile, he always keeps an eye on the compass that leads him to his destination. Follow his example and create the high attraction that inevitably brings you to your destination.

The more detailed you experience everything in your imagination, the more you sense the energy and expectant vitality associated with it. This energy determines your future success. It attracts everything you need to reach your goal: Ideas, outside help and other positive factors such as coincidences and unexpected support.

The most important questions for your vision of the future:

- Where am I and what do I experience in this environment?
- How is my environment designed? What do I see in this place?
- What do I spend my time with – professionally and privately?
- Who am I in contact with? How do I shape my relationships?
- What do I hear and say? How do my conversations and encounters with others go?

Add anything you wish. Leave out anything based on fear, lack or anxiety. Align everything exclusively with the joy and love of your future life.

Use your imagination and these suggestions also for individual sections or projects. Paint the result in detail in connecting pictures and feelings. This will tell you what feels good for you and where you want something too much from your head.

> Anchor your goal with images and feelings and connect with them regularly. Test your imagination with this key question: *How well can I sense my project?*

Intentions: Easier to Results

Many people are setting goals for themselves and then strive to achieve them with lots of effort. This is a high effort, which is also not always crowned with success. There is a simpler way to do this, which also produces even better results: the use of intentions.

Intending Your Future

Let's look at the meaning of that word first. The word comes from Latin and is composed of "in" and "tendere" = pull, stretch, expand, also: aim. "Intention" expresses what it is really about: stretching into something. It signals that we need to stretch ourselves and expand our present borders if we want to achieve something different than we have so far.

What do intentions mean for your goals? Once you have chosen your project and are determined to achieve it, you create an intention. In it you name the path or the result that you really want. Not what you think, that it needs to be done or achieved. Think big and expectant. With your intention you determine what you want to achieve and how you want to get there.

Here are some examples of intentions:

- My earnings exceed my expenses every month.

- My workshops find so much resonance that I have waiting lists for them.

- In ... [city where you live] I experience satisfaction in all areas of my life.

- At the right moment I get all the information I need for my project.

- I arrive safely, quickly and on time /early / at the right time.

The different variants in the last example show how important it is to consider which result you actually want to achieve.

On time, early or at the right time?

Before a seminar I want to arrive early so that I still have enough time for the preparations. Sometimes I also set the exact time.

On the other hand, it is important for me to be at the meeting point in time when I make an appointment. This can also mean that I arrive ten minutes after the agreed date – and this proves to be on time. In the sense that my conversation partner is there for me exactly at this time and I don't have to wait.

You may be surprised that I attach so much importance to precise wording. With your intention, you take a look at what you really want to achieve. The way you put it, you'll get it. Decades ago, scientists used quantum physics to discover that our expectations affect the results. With your intention you set mental expectations that affect your subconscious and your results.

The Subconscious is Like a Little Child

The subconscious can be compared to a small child who cannot interpret, but takes everything literally as it is said – which, incidentally, is the comedy of many children's sayings.

Even our subconscious does not know what we might have meant, but takes us at our word. Therefore, it is important that you name the exact result and the quality of the associated processes – the way you really want them to be.

Intentions are phrased similar to goals and yet differ from them. Well worded goals describe the result as well = *I have arrived!* Intentions, on the other hand, remain somewhat vague, because you don't know how your wish can come about and trust that the best possible way will show up when the time comes – and not a moment earlier. Thus, intentions are missing the important *"This is how it gets there!"* which determine goals.

Structure for Intentions

The following steps are the easiest way to find suitable and powerful intentions:

Topic: For which area or step do you want to set an intention?

Result: What could be the best end result you can imagine? Make sure that you define a result and no measures to get there.

Desired way: What is your wish for the path to the result? This is not about details, but about what *quality* you want to experience.

Wording: Now summarize the result and desired path in a complete sentence.

Three different examples show you how these steps lead to a clear intention.

Easily Complete This Week's Tasks

Topic: complete all tasks that are due this week

Result: all jobs are done at exactly the right time

Desired path: easy and fast

Wording: I complete all tasks of this week in an easy and fast manner. Or: I will complete this week's tasks quickly and easily.

Next, an example from private life:

Having an Enjoyable Holiday

Topic: the last vacation was disturbed by many annoying people

Result: a relaxed holiday with nice people

Desired path: none – it should simply be like this

Wording: We enjoy our holidays with friendly and open-minded people.

And finally, the example of a fledgling business owner:

Winning the First Customer

Topic: not a single customer yet

Result: win my first customer soon

Desired path: different than tried so far; easy to follow

Wording: My first customer comes to me [next week, the week after Easter, Whitsun ...] in an unusual way.

Start with simple topics and gradually increase your demands and expectations. Make sure that your wording meets the following criteria:

Positive Wording

Your subconscious mind looks for the right images for every sentence. If you express something negatively, it cannot find a picture of it and therefore ignores the negation. This leads to you getting what you *don't* want, or reinforcing what you actually want to change.

In the Present Tense

Formulate your intention as if the desired result had already occurred: *That's it!* This means that you leave out everything that "might possibly happen" or what you would have to do or could do for it. Sentences as shown in the examples above are better: *I complete all tasks ... We enjoy our vacation ... My customer finds me ...*

45

Short and Clear

Avoid long sentences. Make sure that you remember your intentions well and that they are clearly worded. This makes it easier for you to use them quickly and on many occasions.

Intentions become flesh and blood over time. Used regularly, they become a very valuable instrument for achieving your goals.

Check Your Intentions Regularly

Write down your sentences. This allows you to check at any time whether and how the desired results have occurred. Compare your wording with reality. In this way, you will learn how to formulate your orientations better and clearer in order to achieve what you want. Here – as in many other areas – the proverb applies: *Practice makes perfect.* At first, the use of intentions is unusual and requires a time of conscious practice to make them an integral part of your everyday life.

Intentions can be formulated for a whole year, for the current month, the current week and the individual day. In addition, you can also use an intention for individual sections of the day. This gives you a clear direction for every period of time – as in the example for a trip to an appointment.

Paving the Way for Ease

With many clients I experience that they are afraid of their own creative power. Even if they have already had good experiences with intentions, they fall back into old habits. They want to check the results as well as individual steps. But control is an illusion and requires a lot of energy. If you let go of your need for control, you can use the energy bound in this control modus for other tasks.

Through our thinking we have it in our hands whether results arise easily or heavily. That doesn't mean everything's going to be the way we want it to be. But most of it is created in a way that suits your project. For this you have to trust that things will develop positively and according to your wishes. This is the only way to create with ease.

Keep your thoughts focused on your vision of the future. If doubts arise, give them an appropriate space. How to deal with doubts, fears and other obstacles and what you need to bear in mind is explained on pages 89 ff.

With intentions you align your wishes to the best result you can imagine. The key question is: *Which result and which path do I really want?*

Commitment: Acting Sensibly

The English term "commitment" is frequently used in other languages as well. That has led to it being used in a more casual, non-committal way as well. When we are talking about commitment with regard to reaching your goals with ease, I prefer to speak of "binding commitment". That better expresses what commitment involves: Commitment plus your willingness to act when the time comes.

With regard to your goals, this means that you first pay attention to what influences your willingness to act. These are primarily your thoughts. They weigh a lot and decide whether you want to do something or not. Your thoughts make you doubt the value of your intentions. They tell you you're not worth realizing your dreams. Whenever you give your limiting thoughts too much space, they gain the upper hand and prevent the desired results from occurring.

On the other hand, thoughts drive us too. They're asking us to get started or do more. They tell us what still needs to be done and how many steps lie ahead. Through your thoughts you get into actionism instead of acting purposefully and taking meaningful steps.

Strengthening the Willingness to Act

Connecting with your project and experiencing yourself in the target situation strengthens your confidence and lets a path emerge in front of your inner eye. What becomes of these inner promptings is determined by your willingness to do something for your project on a regular basis. Not for the sake of action, but in a meaningful way. But how do you recognize when it is time for the next step and which ones makes sense? Include your subconscious.

Task: Retrieve Impulses for Action

Connect with your project so that you can feel it well. Then ask yourself: What step is on the agenda today?

Pay attention to all thoughts and images that appear – no matter how meaningful they seem to you. Write it all down so you can remember it later.

This may seem strange at first. But it works! Try it out and let yourself be surprised by the hints you receive. Do not question emerging impulses, but simply write them down. It's the only way you'll know what's really happening.

Your willingness to constantly do something for your project and to follow your impulses will decide both whether you will reach your goal and how easy it will be to get there.

Results arise when you are willing to follow impulses and act bindingly again and again – even if you do not yet know what the next but one step will be. The key question supports you in this: *To which step do I commit next?*

"Just do it!" Instead of "I Know That!"

I often observe behavior that sabotages my own success and prevents an easy path, as in this example:

Sarah, Participant in a Coaching Group

After the first few meetings in the group, Sarah distances herself more and more from the other participants. When I address it, I hear the following: I am so much further than the others and the exchange with them brings me nothing new. I have been dealing with these topics for years and know them up and down. Her results, however, tell a different story.

A lot of people are like Sarah. They're infested with the "I know that!" syndrome. This is demonstrated by the fact that they have heard or read many things and have dealt extensively with topics and procedures. However, there is a lack of implementation in everyday life. Knowledge alone is not enough to change anything. Only when you put your knowledge into practice and try out new approaches will you be able to see how they actually work and what they achieve. This is not always easy and a new approach can be challenging at times. I would therefore like to take this opportunity to invite you: *Just do it!* The following suggestions will get you moving.

Task: Start Moving

- *Read the procedures described in this chapter again. Choose which of the four tools you want to try within the next 48 hours.*

- *Just take a single point – and put it into practice every day. For at least 28 days. A noticeable change only occurs when you have carried out a new procedure daily (!) at least that long. If you start right away, you'll have results in a month.*

- *Keep a diary during this time. Write down what you intend to do and what experiences you have with it.*

- *Reflect also: What do I expect from it? What is the pressure to actually change anything? Your answers increase your motivation on to stay on the ball.*

- *Take the first step now! Set yourself a date by which you want to have started and one by which you check what has occurred thereby. Do not look at what you are expecting (and that may not happen), but look at what is different than before. This will sharpen your perception and broaden your field of vision.*

- *Find another person and make an agreement about what you want to try out and implement. This will give you a higher level of commitment and a stronger commitment to your own cause. If you link this to a "price tag", i.e. pay a price for doing nothing, the effect can increase further.*

Big changes are easier to implement in small units. The first step is decisive: to decide, to do everything possible and necessary for your own goal. You got to know the tools here. Now it's *"Just do it!"*

Next Steps

Here once again the tools at a glance:

- With your decisiveness, you pave the way.
- By your imagination you anticipate the desired results.
- Intentions support you in getting results faster and easier.
- The binding commitment to your project means that you act sensibly.

Select the tool that has most appealed to you and use it for your project. Try out an approach for at least a week and observe the results: inside you as well as outside. Take an expectant, curious attitude.

ENTRUST YOURSELF TO THE RIVER

For many people, the thought that it might be easy to reach their goal is initially disturbing. Most of them learned as children that if you want to achieve something, you have to work hard. Therefore, negative memories emerge at first when I address this topic in speeches or workshops.

While some of you wish that things could be different, others strongly resist this idea. *That can't be!* Then much of what you have learned so far or how you have proceeded would have been wrong. This must be digested before you can get used to the idea that it could be different.

> The need to stay in control is an important factor that makes it difficult to experience more ease.

Because we experience a high degree of uncertainty in many areas, there is a great need to have things under control in at least one area. This seems possible with one's own goals – even if the path may be long and hard. You anticipate it and adjust to it. And you're supposed to change that now, trust in the flow of life and let yourself drift?!

Yes! At least try it out. Experience what it's like. With each step and each further experience, it becomes easier. Until you have taken it to heart: *That's really possible – and it's even faster!*

Believing in Your Success

Starting point for a change of your usual approach to acting are your previous successes. They support you in believing that you can realize your project and achieve your highest goals. Now I hear from some people: *I've had no success in my life. Everything just went by itself.* I don't think so, because success is a question of perspective.

You are reading this book, and this is the first small proof that there have been some successes in your life: You have learned to read – not a self-evident fact, as more than seven million illiterates in Germany prove. You have probably finished school and at least one apprenticeship. You have undertaken and prepared journeys. You have already changed a lot in your life – this can also be booked to the success account. It is not important that you are proud of the result, but that you are aware of the results that have occurred as a product of your actions. This allows you to connect the dots between a starting point – what has moved you to change something – and an endpoint, namely what happens through your actions – that is, a success.

Find Evidence in Your Own Life

Look back and lift the treasure that is in your past experiences. And as is the case with a treasure hunt, this can take some time. This is especially true when you see past changes as something that has happened to you and over which you have had no influence. But there are also more treasures to be discovered than you initially suspect. Bring them to the surface.

Task: Searching for Clues

Walk mentally through your life and look for previous suc-
cesses. On the success account you can book everything you
have started and finished, no matter whether you enjoyed it
or not. Think also of

- *school, training and further education – with or without a*
  degree,

- *defeats from which you have emerged strengthened,*

- *activities that you have undertaken on your own initiative*
  and in which you have learned something.

What motivated you or held you by the bar to finish what you
had begun? What thoughts or beliefs did support you?

For example, sentences like these: When I set my mind on
something, I reach it too ... I don't let go until I have achieved
something ... When I know what I want, nothing can stop me
anymore ...

It's those affirmative sentences you're looking for. Usually we
are not at all aware of the potential in these thoughts, also
called "convictions" or "beliefs". With your search for clues you
can recognize them and use them consciously. If things don't
go the way you want them to, if obstacles arise, or if you have
no idea how to go on, these sentences will help you to stay
your ground.

Finding Role Models

A second factor for staying on track is role models: People who
have already achieved what we cannot yet imagine. Keep on

looking for shining examples that encourage you to believe that you can achieve your goals as well. Negative examples are always available from the media and your environment. However, they prevent you from finding your own path and from courageously walking it.

In contrast, role models prove that there are possibilities to realize one's own dreams. They show us that challenges are part of the road and that we can grow with them. They give us examples for our own actions and motivate us to stick to our dreams and follow our ideas. Both celebrities and normal people, whose stories you have witnessed, are suitable for this. It could just as well be a novel character or a historical personality about whom you have read something. You can learn from all of them how they found their path and constantly pursued it. They will also tell you what obstacles they encountered and how they overcame them. And you recognize that resistance strengthens you and leads you to discover new pathways and to consolidate your own will.

That doesn't mean you have to do it the same way your role models do. That would just make you a bad copy. It is more important to derive ideas for your own approach, your willpower and implementation strength. You'll still have to go your own way. But the experiences of others show you that and how it becomes possible for you to achieve your goals.

Let Yourself be Guided

The need for control is one of the biggest obstacles if you want to get anywhere easily. This allows you to stay in the familiar grid and always use the same procedure because it is familiar. But perhaps there is a way for you that would be simpler, more effective and therefore also faster? Since you don't know it yet, you can't take it either.

So, you need an advisor or an authority you can trust that has access to all the information that will help you go another way. How do you find this guide?

One thing's for sure, it's not your mind. It can only access on what you have already experienced, processed and stored in the brain. Only a small part of the thousands of information of a single day ends up there. Before this, they pass through a sluice in which they are filtered on the basis of previous experience and classified as important or unimportant. This means that you only have a very small part of what is important for your goals and an easy way to get there.

You receive the decisive clues from another level: from collective consciousness. Here we have all the information we need to make our dreams come true and easily reach our goals. We get the connection to this through our inner counsellor – also called "intuition" – that can draw from this knowledge and make it available to us. Do it like all really successful people and let yourself be guided by this counsellor.

Trust the Inner Counselor

In earlier times, before decisions were made, all available information was collected, weighed against each other or pro and contra lists were written. Today you do research on the Internet until your head smokes, and in the end you're no smarter than before. The inner counsellor helps us to make the right decisions for the situation. When we listen to its advice, it gently and consistently guides us on the best path to our goal.

Every human being has an inner counselor. However, the access may be buried. Let's open this door again.

Task: Tracking Down Your Inner Counsellor

Over the next few days, pay conscious attention to the small, often only short impulses that appear when you have formulated an intention. How do you perceive them? Is it a feeling? Or do you have a recurring thought? Do you hear an inner voice? Or do you simply know what to do – even if you cannot explain it to yourself?

Write these impulses down. They appear as ideas, sentences or also in the form of calls to action, such as the thought "Call XY!"

Follow these instructions and check what results they produce.

Your inner counsellor makes itself known in different ways. It can talk to you, deliver pictures or give impulses through feelings. Sometimes it provides information on all channels to attract your attention. In the beginning, some attention is needed to distinguish its clues from your usual thoughts. Trust that impulses will return if you do not recognize them immediately. Or ask that you receive information in a way that you understand.

For contact with your inner counselor, you need to let go of control and accept the hints instead of questioning whether they are right, what they bring, or what comes out of them. Follow your hints for a few weeks and write down what happens. You will notice that in the course of time a positive strengthening cycle develops: pay attention to impulses – follow the guidance – gain trust – receive further hints.

Become Indifferent

So far you have already taken important steps: You have set yourself a goal, found a name and a symbol for it. You have experienced how you repeatedly connect with your goal and keep it in mind. These steps gradually create an emotional connection to your project, from which you gain the strength and courage to act. But this close connection also holds a danger: You are no longer indifferent in the sense that every possibility is equally valid – and thus you lose the light-heartedness with which you *easily* reach your goal.

Avoid the "How"

You probably know the first stumbling block very well: the stronger you want something, the faster the question appears: *How can it go?* Basically, this question is justified and, in some instances, it will bring results. Asked too early, however, it quickly brings your project prematurely to a end. For two reasons:

- You begin to plan the path to the goal and define individual steps. This is the most commonly used approach and the classic way. These plans are only a repetition of tried and tested procedures. They rarely show the best or even the easiest way to achieve results. Instead of starting with the big picture and involving your inner counselor, you go into details. It's easy for you to fall into blind actionism. True to the motto *"Be active!"*

- You begin to doubt your project, especially if it is larger than or different from your previous goals. At the beginning, you have no idea how to implement it. This opens the door to doubt. With the question of "how" these are additionally fed. Already at the first obstacle you start to sway. Many see it as a sign that it is the wrong goal or that they will not make it. Often, questions such as these – usually harmlessly meant – are added from the environment: *Have you thought this through completely?* Or: *How are you going to do that?* In such circumstances it takes a very firm belief in one's own goal to stay on and not give up.

If you catch yourself thinking about the "how", tell yourself: *The how will show itself while walking!* Then ask yourself the question: *What exactly do I want to achieve?* With it you get out of the threatening negative spiral and align yourself again to your project.

Let go of Emotional Attachment

The intensive preoccupation with one's own project almost in-evitably leads to a close emotional connection with it. We want it so badly and we're willing to do anything to make it happen. This is very positive at first, but it reduces the probability of reaching your goal easily. You are so preoccupied with your goal and the possibilities of how to get there that you don't recognize emerging opportunities or dismiss them as inappro-priate. They stand in your way and make life harder for you than it should be.

The difficulty arises from the fact that you are emotionally too strongly attached to your project. You are stuck to your idea of what the result should look like and how to get there. You have a tunnel vision and filter all possibilities according to whether they fit to your ideas or not. Even if chances were presented on the proverbial silver platter, you would not accept them and would reject them as unattractive.

Only when you let go of your attachment do new paths open up that take you to your destination faster and easier, as this personal example shows:

A new Website in a Weekend

For quite some time I had felt that my web appearance no longer fit me. In spring, I talked to my web designer about it and agreed with her that she would create an interim solution that could be easily adapted later. As I was involved in other projects, further steps were delayed. I had set myself a goal: At the beginning of October my new appearance is online.

I asked for offers for the graphic design – and couldn't decide on anyone. So, I put the matter aside again. In the meantime, I had let go of all expectations about the result and the path to it and trusted that a good solution would be found. Ten days before the planned date, I decided to go online with the interim solution.

In the preparatory discussion, a possibility arose which I had not considered until then: my web designer suggested that I make a draft for the visual design I wanted so that she would get an idea of my expectations. That same afternoon I received her draft and was thrilled. Over the weekend, we put all pieces together. On Monday night, everything was ready to go online. Both the website and the blog got a new look, which is exactly what I had wished for.

There are many ways to let go of the emotional attachment to the result. I have had particularly good experiences with the Sedona method. Search online for details and access to materials or trainings.

Learn All you Need to Know About Your Project

This may sound like a contradiction to the last point, but it is not. The more you know about your project, the easier it will be to implement it. You expand your perception and discover possibilities that you did not know before. You talk to people about your project and thereby discover more and other aspects of it.

Research

Find out how your role models proceeded. How did they come up with their idea? What did they do? Who helped them? What tools did they use? Especially in blogs you will find many stories and case studies in which people describe how they managed to achieve certain goals.

Since we can easily lose ourselves in the diversity of information when surfing the Internet, limit the time you want to spend and set yourself an alarm clock. At the beginning, set yourself an intention with which you control your research. Here are some suggestions: *I find an instruction for ... I discover new possibilities, how ... My research brings me new knowledge/motivation/contacts...*

Collect everything you come across – even if you don't need it until later or never.

Brainstorming

In some places, brainstorming, i.e. finding creative ideas, is helpful, for instance if you want to find out which basic steps and paths lead to your goal. Perhaps you also need ideas for your project as a whole or for the next steps. Or you are facing a problem for which you are looking for solutions. You can brainstorm classically in a group of three to four people or you do it by yourself.

In addition to people who already know your project well, choose people who are unfamiliar with the matter. In this way you get both a neutral view of your goal as well as surprising suggestions, because these people are not familiar with it and therefore see it differently.

The task for your idea generation process should be as simple and yet as specific as possible. The clearer you formulate the task, the more varied and better the results will be. Define the topic in a neutral, clear form and without anticipating answers.

Although brainstorming is first and foremost a group method, it can also be done on your own. Here are a few suggestions:

Exercise: Finding New Ideas on Your Own

Put yourself in another identity. Think about how this person would solve your problem or – if it is a historical figure – would have solved it. Possible identities are: a Stone Age person, an astronaut, a person of the opposite sex, well-known personalities such as Albert Einstein, George Clooney, the Dalai Lama or Chancellor Angela Merkel.

Also look at your problem from the point of view of another habitat: How would it be seen at the North Pole? In the South Seas? On the moon?

Bring in another epoch: What does the situation look like if you take it back 1,500 years? To the Renaissance? The year 2050?

Recognize the Next Step

As long as you want to stay in control of the route and approach, there is a risk that you will act ill-considered and force results. This rarely works and quickly leads to frustration and doubt. As soon as you have adopted a neutral attitude of expectation towards your goal, i.e. have become indifferent / valid, you can act purposefully. That includes doing nothing and waiting for the next impulse.

How can you tell whether it is time to act and what steps are to be taken? By pausing regularly, connecting with your goal and allowing yourself to be guided to the next step. The following procedure can also be used to review planned steps:

Ritual to Recognize the Next Step

Turn inside once a day for about 15 minutes. Take a few deep breaths and relax with each breath. Formulate an intention. For instance: I clearly see the next step. *Or:* The next step shows itself to me ... (light/fast/clearly).

Get in touch with your project and put yourself in the desired target situation. Ask the question: What is the next step (today)?

Pay attention to all impulses and do not censor anything. Write down everything that appears – and be prepared to follow these impulses.

You can use the question to check steps you have already planned: Is this the right next step? *The better you are connected with your inner counselor, the clearer you will perceive the answers.*

Regularly used, this time of connecting to your inner counsellor becomes a valuable ritual, through which you get faster and clearer clues for your next steps. Furthermore, you can ask questions in all important situations during the day, such as: *What's important now?* Or: *What should I pay attention to?* Over time, you will realize how well connected you are with your inner counselor and use its helpful hints.

Next Steps

- Use these steps to strengthen your trust – in yourself, in your inner counselor and in additional support for your path.

- Write down any results and insights and see what works and how. This enhances your feeling secure about your further steps.

PROGRESSING FASTER WITH SUPPORT

When cigarette advertising was still allowed on television, there he was: the Marlboro Man. The lonely horseman, who heroically met all dangers with his herd of cattle and mastered them. He stands as a symbol for the lonely fighters who believe that they don't need anyone and can best achieve their goals on their own. That may be true. The fact is, however, that it is much faster with the support of others. All successful people know that.

Andrew Carnegie, American Steel Baron

The highly successful entrepreneur is an excellent example of what can be achieved with mutual support. We know from him that he met weekly in a Mastermind group with other entrepreneurs. Following the same structure every time, they encouraged each other to implement ambitious projects and realize their entrepreneurial visions.

Even if your destination is a few sizes smaller, take Andrew Carnegie as your role model. Find people who support you on your personal path – and for whom you do the same.

What Support Does

What would we be without motivating companions that are at our side when courage leaves us? From these people we receive encouragement and confirmation for our dreams, visions and goals. With them we also succeed in the seemingly impossible, because they confirm us in our ideas and endure it when we overflow with enthusiasm. They encourage us to go on and enter unfamiliar territory so that we come closer to our dreams. They challenge us to recognize our self-defined boundaries and help us to question and transcend them. They show us paths when we have lost our way in the undergrowth of our thoughts and do not know what to do. With their support, we dare to take steps that previously seemed too big and unfeasible. And they challenge us to take small, concrete steps, make agreements with us on this and make sure that we keep to them.

All this is possible – if you choose your companions well. Check for yourself whether you are a source of inspiration, motivation and encouragement for others as well.

The Three Levels of Support

In addition to being accompanied and motivated by other people, it is also important to find encouragement in oneself. Because there's not always someone available when you need help. In addition, you can also request support from the universe.

Level 1: Finding Support Within Yourself

What enables you to remain in good spirits even when things are not going as you would like them to? At times like these, it's crucial that you have access to something that strengthens you. Those are your thoughts, on the one hand. These have an enormous impact on how you master difficult situations, deal with defeats and remain confident. Reinforcement can also come from an inner place of power to which you can go again and again. This is a place in nature or in a house, where you can retreat mentally to recharge your batteries.

Task: Designing Your Personal Place of Power

- *Find a place where you feel completely well and where you like to be (place of power). Notice this place in all its details (see, hear, feel).*

- *What is there to see where you actually are? Now go mentally to your place of power and see what there is to see at this place.*

- *What is to be heard in the place where you are at the moment? Change to your place of power and hear what can be heard there.*

- *What can you smell in the place where you are right now? Now go to your place of power and smell what there is to smell at this place.*

- *Feel how the chair you are sitting on carries you and how your feet touch the ground. Go to your place of power and feel what there is to feel at this place.*

- *Let your breath ascend and descend in the pleasant atmosphere of your place of power and experience this as a process of holding on and letting go.*

- *Imagine how you let the flow of air rise through your spine when you inhale and how it leaves your body through your forehead.*

- *Imagine at the end how energy flows through you and you return to the place where you really are with this energy flow and how you powerfully go into your next stage of the day.*

▪ *Before you direct your attention outward, imagine how the day evolves in contact with this energy.*

Another source of power is your inner counsellor, which you have already got to know. You can trust it at any time and ask it for advice and support.

Rituals can also be used to create constructive habits that give you energy and ease your path. This can be the daily ritual already described, in which you connect with your project, formulate an intention for the day and get hints for your next steps. In addition, there are numerous other options that will strengthen you.

Supporting Rituals: Examples

▪ *Prepare a special tea. When you're drinking it, think about what's next and how to proceed.*

▪ *Visualize daily for ten minutes how it will be when you reached your goal.*

▪ *Create an alter ego, a kind of creative self that has all the qualities you need. Ask your alter ego how you can master challenges, or engage in a dialogue with it about your next steps.*

▪ *Literally take a different angle. Lie upside down on your bed with your feet facing your headboard. Look at the world from this different perspective. Or create a special place dedicated only to your goal.*

- *Go to a café one fixed day a week. Develop ideas there on how to achieve your project even better.*

- *Start the day dancing. For example, with a CD that links music with affirmations or reassuring texts.*

Level 2: Support from Other People

As varied as people are their needs and preferences. Where one person prefers to work alone and only seeks selective support, for others a continuous ex-change with a high degree of commitment is important. Support groups, which also exist in the form of tandems – i.e. meetings of only two people – are ideal for this purpose. Groups of four to six people are particularly stimulating and effective. Support groups can be found under different names; their approach is usually very similar. Here are the most important characteristics:

Success Team

Success teams are small personal networks in which people support each other in achieving their goals and becoming more successful. They exist as groups facilitated by a coach and as self-organized groups.

Mastermind Group

The term "mastermind" (among other things a synonym for God) indicates that this form of support originally had a spiritual orientation. This has watered down in the meantime. However, these groups are still concerned with following the eight master-mind principles that are read out at the beginning of each meeting. One of them is: *I serve God and men in a way that gives others an example worth imitating, and judge myself according to the leadership of a higher power.*

In contrast to success teams, the focus here is not only on personal growth and the achievement of goals, but also on a "successful and happy life in every respect".

Encouragement Group

In this form developed by me, elements from the other two groups combine. I know these from the experience of personal participation as well as from more almost 25 years of accompanying successful teams, which I have initiated regularly.

These groups work with the elements of the Encouraging Principle described in this book, which can be applied to any type of goal. The participants encourage each other to integrate this approach into their everyday lives, to take significant steps on a regular basis and to act in a binding manner.

Level 3: Request Support from the Universe

Finally, there is this third level, to which more and more people are returning or finding a new access. In universal consciousness all knowledge is available that we need for our personal path. On the one hand, we have access to it through our inner counsellor, who is an ideal mediator for it. On the other hand, meditation and contemplation also serve to connect with it and to receive information about it. Also strengthening, so-called affirmative prayers connect us with universal wisdom and direct our attention to what we desire. With them we express that we trust that everything comes to us "in its time and form" – and gratefully accept this.

We experience the support from this level as coincidence, as hints from within and outside or as clear knowledge of what we have to do or what is right and important for us.

You can further support this by asking for it in your daily ritual or in connection with your inner counselor: *Show me the perfect solution.* Ask specifically for what you need. Meditate, connect to your inner self and pay attention to which pictures, ideas or other hints appear.

Finding the Right Companions

No matter whether you are looking for a companion in a tandem or a group: Choosing the right people is important for a successful cooperation. First find out what your needs and expectations are and what is important to you. At this point, be absolutely honest with yourself. Your – even unspoken – expectations determine the results of the search and selection of your future companions. Only if you know what you want and expect from your companions will you find the right people.

Start your search with the people around you. With them it is easier for you to assess what qualities they bring to a collaboration. Who is so pleasant that you can imagine a regular exchange? Who is determined, willing to change and positive in their basic attitude? Talk to these people about your desire for continuous exchange and mutual support. It quickly becomes clear who are actually interested and want to pursue their own goals consistently.

In your conversations, make sure that the following factors also apply.

Criteria for Selection

Sympathy is only one – and not even the most important – aspect for the selection of your companions. Much more important are these four factors as they have a greater impact on possible outcomes:

Willingness to Change

Surround yourself with people who are really willing to actively shape their lives and change situations that no longer fit. Also check your own attitude to change, because your attitude attracts exactly those people who resonate with you. The greater your own willingness, the easier it will be for you to attract people who also invest time and energy in their own development and want to achieve contentment, joy of life and well-being.

Commitment in Acting

The willingness to change is one thing. But without commitment to act it remains without effect. Only in the combination do the strength and the will emerge to regularly and actively take committed steps towards one's own goals.

Ask your future companions how they deal with adverse circumstances right at the first meeting: *How long do you stay on and what has to happen for you to give up?* Check this point for yourself: Do obstacles quickly lead you away from your plans or are you looking for ways and means to overcome them?

Openness for Suggestions and New Ideas

A trustful cooperation is characterized by the fact that everyone opens up and also talks about points that they find unpleasant or tricky. This is only possible if everyone – at least little by little – drops their visor and refrains from presenting themselves with a supposedly perfect self-image. This cannot be maintained anyway, because in tandem or in a group you can only hide your supposed weaknesses for a short time. Here you get to know each other very well with your preferences and peculiarities as well as your strengths and weaknesses.

This makes it possible to support each other in a way that brings out the best in everyone. It also means that we hear how others perceive us, where they see our strengths, what they notice and what suggestions they have for our development. Who finds it difficult to accept ideas and hints from others – and that is not always easy! – will also keep their own perception behind the curtain and thus withhold important clues from the other members.

On the other hand, those who are open to something new are usually willing to go into unknown areas of thought, and can thus literally engage in the "unheard of".

Trust in the Power of Community

With the right people, a power of implementation emerges that cannot be developed alone. Then the team resembles a power plant that provides the energy for change and a high drive to advance all pro-jects. Together they create a special spirit that affects everyone. This allows great things to come into being because new thoughts are thought, expressed and developed jointly. Together, the existing is enlarged and something un-common is created. This gives rise to new opportunities that serve all those involved and advance each individual on his or her own path.

When Silence is Appropriate

Even if you have just heard the praise of the potentials of mu-tual support, there are situations, in which silence is appropri-ate. This is the case if a project or an idea is still too precious for you and you feel that any form of criticism would destroy your still young and sensitive seedling of thought. Even if you have agreed to confidentiality in your group, you should only bring in plans and ideas that really make you feel comfortable and that will not be harmed if somebody does talk to you.

In such cases, stop for a moment and ask yourself: *Do I really want to share this?* Your first impulse counts – pay attention to it before your mind tells you otherwise. It is always better to tell something once too late than to feel sorry for a long time afterwards.

A Beneficial Structure for Your Meetings

Once you have assembled your support team, a clear structure will help you use your time effectively and achieve best results. Two aspects are in the foreground:

- to support each other in easily achieving their personal goals;

- to reflect on the previous approach and to adapt it in such a way that desired changes are initiated and objectives achieved.

The structure presented here supports you in implementing these two points and working together as efficiently and smoothly as possible. It consists of three parts:

Initial Round

Start each meeting – whether on the phone, online or in person – with all members reporting on their progress and their state of affairs. The following questions serve as a guide for this first five-minute round:

- How did I complete the steps I committed to (see below)?

- What have I achieved by that?

- What experiences were associated with these steps?

- What insights have I gained?

If you prepare for this round in advance, the meeting will proceed swiftly.

Support Phase

This part is at the core of your team work. You will get suggestions and help from the group to advance your project. Here two key points will help you to prepare yourself and achieve the best possible result.

- Briefly describe your current situation or present a topic you are dealing with. At the end give an "order" to the group, which results from this question: *Which support do I need and wish for my next step?*

- The group members now contribute ideas, tips, questions, methods or solutions. Limit this round to 15 minutes per person for five or six members, or 20 minutes for up to four participants. This time frame should be monitored by a timekeeper.

Here, too, efficiency is highest if you already come to the meeting prepared with your most important topic.

Commitment

At the end of the meeting, everyone defines at least one concrete step, which they are willing to commit to implementing until the next time. No ifs or buts. This can be a point from the support phase or something more important.

To check the level of your commitment to fulfill your promise, ask yourself the following question: *On a scale of 1 -10, how committed am I for this?* If your answer is less than 10 choose another step for which you are willing to give your best.

The more committed you are in delivering on your promises, the better and faster you will achieve results with the help of your team.

Agree on what happens if you do not fulfill what you have committed to. This could be a financial contribution, which comes into a common piggy bank. Often unfinished tasks show that there is something wrong with the subproject or related topics. This can also happen with tasks that cannot be completed within the agreed time, such as *I am up to date with my files*. Or the subject has arisen in your mind and feelings associated with it have not been considered.

Next Steps

▪ Find at least one person with whom you can arrange to support each other for an initial period of three months. At the end of this time you decide if and how you want to continue.

▪ Be committed in your actions. Don't make excuses – neither with yourself nor with the other members of your team. Question any justifications put forward that prevent you or others from acting.

▪ Observe what is happening or changing by working together. Pay special attention to surprising results, changes in your energy level and feedback from your environment.

EASE AGAIN AND AGAIN

We were born with a sense of ease as our birthright. While some people stay connected to it for the rest of their lives, others lose access and have to find it again. Remember your childhood and how easy it was to enter other worlds. We imagined what it looked like there, experienced adventures that we had thought up or played out ourselves and were able to master all the challenges as easy as child's play. At least in our imagination.

This ease is lost to us over the years and with it also the access to how we easily realize dreams. The good news is we can find that access again. This is easier said than done, but not impossible. The suggestions in this chapter will help you.

Ease is a Choice

You choose all day long – and act most of the time on autopilot. You choose to always take the same route to work. You choose to complete your tasks in the same way every time. You choose to think the same thoughts in 90% of the time. Even if you are not aware of it, you choose what to do and leave something else for it. And thus, you arrive at the same results over and over again.

As long as these choices fit you, everything's fine. But if you are not satisfied with the results (anymore) or the path to achieving them is too exhausting, you need a different strategy. In order to develop a new strategy and gradually implement it, it is important to know how you act habitually and how you make life difficult for yourself. Find out what ease means to you and how it is created.

What Does "Ease" Actually Mean?

"Ease" means something different to every human being. This is also shown by the answers I received to the question *"What do you associate with ease?"*

- When thoughts and answers come by themselves.
- The opposite of heavy.
- That something happens without effort.
- To be able to switch off permanent worries and fears, at least sometimes.
- There's nothing to do just to be!
- To concentrate on the goal instead of the thought carousel in my head.
- To be in the present moment with a clear head and my whole heart.

As you can see, ease is often defined in contrast to what we perceive as the opposite – heaviness, effort, worry. For others, it is a feeling that arises when they are in a state of flow and in harmony with themselves and their goal, and when things fit in, or happen "by themselves".

Task: How do You Define Ease?

Define ease for yourself. To do this, finish the following sentence with a pictorial description: Ease is like ...

Here are some examples: ... to float like weightlessly in warm water ... to be carried by strong arms ... a constantly bubbling source ...

With a pictorial description you gain positive access to your personal understanding of ease. Perhaps there is a symbol in this image or metaphor that helps you to remember again and again to pursue your goals with more ease.

How Ease is Developed

Every change begins with a thought: *I want to change X and reach Y.* This is the starting point from which you move. Once you have decided – another thought! –, you start thinking about how you will reach your goal. Whether the individual steps will be associated with hardship or easy for you, your mind has a decisive influence on that. And that brings us to an important point.

Ease starts in the mind and can be perceived in the body.

For the most part, your thoughts determine how much ease you experience on the path to your goal.

Ease Starts in Your Mind

Do you know what you really think about your goals and the path there? Probably not. Pay attention to your thoughts, because they are the key to more ease. Even if we really want something, there are voices within us who are against it and are doing everything they can to undermine our success. This inner dialogue between proponents and opponents, however, is rarely perceived. Therefore, it is essential to get to the bottom of one's own thoughts.

Task: What are you Thinking?

What did the passage you just read triggered in you? Take a piece of paper and write all the thoughts that have just come to your mind.

Which of these do you consider as positive and constructive and which as negative and restrictive?

At first, it is only a matter of starting to consciously pay attention to your thoughts. Thoughts are very fleeting, so it's helpful to write them down. Keep pausing every now and then while you are working on your project and pay attention to what you think about your goals and the chances of achieving them. Find out which sentences support you on your path and which inhibit you in your activities. Your body helps you to recognize this.

Every Thought has a Resonance in the Body

Most people are so driven by their thoughts that they have lost perception of their body and its signals. Your body is a perfect sensor and shows you what state of mind you are in right now. However, you will recognize this only if you pause and consciously perceive your body's signals. And that is exactly where the challenge lies!

At first it is difficult for us to get out of our accustomed way of thinking and to perceive our body signals – but it can be trained.

Exercise: What do you Perceive in Your Body Right Now?

Stop reading, take a deep breath and consciously move from the head to the rest of your body. What do you notice there?

Do not evaluate your perception, but only take note of what you notice: ... heart beat ... a strong pulsation ... pressure in the head ... cold or warm hands/feet ...

Stay with your attention and keep watching what happens. What remains the same, what changes?

Every thought has a resonance in your body. Therefore, your body can also signal to you whether your thoughts are beneficial (pleasant) or obstructive (unpleasant). Thus, it also reflects in which mental-emotional state you are at the moment: Ease or strain?

Our thoughts are the trigger for many things. They influence whether we do something or are not; they support our actions or make them more difficult. They make us think big or keep us small. All this can be determined by body perception, as the following experiment shows.

Exercise: Feeling Your Thoughts

Take a few deep breaths until you have arrived with your attention completely at yourself and in the present.

In each of the following sentences, pay attention to where in your body you feel a resonance. It's not about what you think about them and whether you agree with the content or not. Only pay attention to what happens on the physical level while thinking these statements.

- *Life is beautiful.*
- *Life is exhausting.*
- *Everything's fine.*
- *I've got everything I need.*
- *I have to ... (complete what you currently have to do, for example: ... file the tax return)*
- *I should ... (add a point, for example: ... call/visit my mother/father)*

Can you perceive differences between the different statements? If this is not yet the case, try it again and again. Over time, you will recognize subtle differences in perception.

This exercise can be used for your further steps to your goal. Regularly check what a thought, idea or approach feels like. With a little practice, you'll be able to recognize which steps feel easy and which don't. In interplay with the hints of your inner counsellor, you develop your own personal yardstick that shows you the path that suits you best.

Use the knowledge that you can recognize the quality of your thoughts through your body to achieve your goals. This key question supports you in this: How does it feel?

Gaining Ease

If you know what ease means to you, you can decide for yourself how you want to design your path, instead of continuing to follow the standards of others. Your own ideas are the only guideline. You alone determine the speed at which you implement your project. You decide when you to drift in the river and where you want to take the paddles back into your hand and increase the number of strokes. For your decision you have a clever advisor: your body.

Strengthen Body Awareness

As already mentioned, your body is the best sensor to measure the amount of ease you (want to) experience. Through it you will learn how to reach your destination in a suitable way. Like a constantly bubbling spring, your body continuously sends clues: *This is good for you ... This feels strange ... Something is wrong ...* Even if you don't pay attention, you get signals who and what is right / wrong, consistent / incongruous, beneficial / harmful for you and your life.

We got this gift – so we can use it. With babies and toddlers this knowing can still be observed very well: They turn to some people and reject others. Unfortunately, we are being trained to discard this ability at an early stage. Whenever we expressed our perception, we heard sentences like: *You're imagining things! ... Don't say that! ... That's not true! ... You're crazy!* No wonder, then, that we no longer trust the clues of our bodily perception.

Feeling Instead of Thinking

Those who have forgotten to rely on their own feelings easily have the impression that they cannot feel anything. That's not true, it just takes practice. Little by little you will regain access to recognize the signals of your body and understand their meaning.

Access to my Inner Treasure Chest

For many years I could not perceive my feelings. I was so much in my head that I no longer had access to other parts of my body. This changed in a training course in which feeling played an important role. The trainer showed me with a simple exercise that I felt all the time. However, my feeling was so subtle that it took me some time to recognize it without my thoughts immediately taking control over it. Without noticing it, I had adopted the childhood devaluation of my perceptions and thus misplaced the key to my personal treasure chest.

Be aware of how quickly you evaluate your perceptions. Here are some examples: *Such nonsense! ... What do I imagine again – He (she/it) is perfectly in order! ... I've got another crazy idea ... Where is it coming from?! ...* It is sentences like these that habitually appear and torpedo your perception.

Perceiving Instead of Interpreting

You regain access to your body wisdom by simply beginning to perceive what a thought, place or event feels like – without label, evaluation, assessment or description. Simply:

Interesting! That's what it feels like! In this way, you recognize what energy is contained in it and understand it as your own hidden power. This energy can be used with increasing practice on many occasions.

What we commonly call "feelings" are in fact emotions. Feelings are pure, unfiltered body perception. In contrast, emotions arise when we interpret and evaluate experiences. These do not correspond to the real body perception because they have been enlarged, distorted or generalized. This leads to your acting in a predictable way in similar situations. Your interpretation influences your view of certain experiences and recurring events. Try it out for yourself.

Exercise: Fear or Excitement?

Bring back a situation you considered unpleasant. Remember what you perceived in your body. Without interpretation these body sensations are mostly: damp palms, faster heartbeat, flat breathing, shaky knees ...

Next, think of a situation where you were excited about something important to you. What body perception did you have in this situation? Without interpretation these are usually: damp palms, faster heartbeat, flat breathing, shaky knees...

You see: The pure body perception is very similar in both situations. The only difference is your interpretation and the label you give to each occasion: Once it is: I'm scared! *The second time:* How exciting!

86

It is precisely in these labels that the problem lies – and at the same time the solution: instead of judging or evaluating what appears, we only notice without and let it be.

Rename Experiences Differently

Get used to speaking more about the exciting situations that you have experienced (and mastered), and less about the fear that was your companion. You will notice over time how this changes your behavior and makes you more courageous. Re-naming or re-framing a situation changes your point of view and increases your options. That is a decisive factor!

From a neutral, non-judgmental position it is easier to stick to a feeling. Normally we get out of an un-pleasant perception as quickly as possible and flee into thinking. Without evaluation you can fully experience the feeling in your body. You will dis-cover the vibration contained in every feeling and experience how it pulsates powerfully through your body.

Labelling something limits and controls this force. Without judgement, you gain greater freedom – in feeling, in acting, and in your ability to shape your life in a way that is appropri-ate, coherent, and easy for you.

When Everything's Just Heavy

Still, sometimes everything just feels heavy. Then it is not a solution to run up against a brick wall or to put yourself under pressure with sentences like *That just has to be NOW!* In-stead, take a step back.

Exercise: How Could it Go Easier?

This question changes your focus. Away from the heaviness you feel towards possibilities for experiencing more ease.

Set a timer to three minutes and ask yourself: How could it go easier? *Find at least ten ideas of what you can do or not do right now to make "it" (your condition, the task at hand, your project) easier.*

You'll be surprised at how many possibilities there are. Due to the tight time schedule, even seemingly crazy ideas come to paper. Among them are usually a few useful ones, which you can implement. If you find that you take your project far too seriously and still lack a little playful ease, you can also develop a few ideas for that.

Next Steps

- Pay attention to your body's signals and accept its clues. Check your steps: Does this step feel easy? How could it be any easier?

- Trust in the flow of life and let yourself drift. Enjoy your journey to your destination.

FLOW AROUND OBSTACLES ELEGANTLY

As soon as you start your trip to your destination, they show up: Obstacles, blockages and ghosts of the past. They are natural companions on the road to your goal and simply belong to it when we break new ground. It is not only hesitant or anxious people who experience that something gets in their way. Even if you start with self-confidence and great enthusiasm, you will experience moments when you can't get any further. Many people are discouraged by this, which is a pity – after all, there are procedures with which you remain capable of acting or become capable again.

Obstacles appear in ourselves in the form of fears and doubts or as resistances and unwillingness. From the outside they come in the form of hurdles of any kind or as critical voices from the environment. In both cases, the point is to see them for what they are: Signposts and ambassadors.

What Obstacles Tell Us

First and foremost, obstacles show us that there is a need for clarification. When we enter unknown territory, they signal that caution is required. We must first learn what is normal and whether our usual procedures can be applied here. Therefore, it is important that you acknowledge that encountering obstacles, resistances and blockages is normal and part of growth and change. Only then will you find ways and means to reach your destination.

Clarification: What Kind of Obstacle?

Find out what this is about: Is it fear or doubt? Do you feel internal resistance? These can also manifest themselves as paralysis or unwillingness.

Or do you experience resistance from outside? These can be critical remarks from your environment that throw you off track, as well as bureaucratic or practical limitations.

Whether criticism from your environment is a mirror of your inner state or the personal subject of the other person can easily be determined if you follow Elisabeth Kübler-Ross's advice: *"Everything that occupies us for more than ten minutes are our own unsolved issues."* When you realize that it is your own topic, consider critical remarks as a gift to gain further certainty and clarity.

Obstacles Challenge Us

Obstacles show us that we cannot implement our ideas so easily. Instead, they request us

- to deal with them: In this way we can recognize what is behind them and accept the clues they contain. Since most obstacles arise in the mind, it is important that you look at, review and adapt your basic beliefs.

- to question our goals: How committed am I? Is that what I really want? Am I on the right track? Do I want too much – or perhaps too little?

- not to resist or react stubbornly, but to become creative and find an easier way: How to play with obstacles is explained below.

- to become or remain capable of acting despite existing fears and emerging doubts: This can also mean accepting that nothing is going on at the moment and taking a break from your goal.

Review Your Beliefs

As already mentioned elsewhere, everything in life is created twice: First, your thoughts form an idea, which in the second step emerges in reality. The same applies to obstacles. They, too, are first created as a thought and then appear as a mirror image in reality. Therefore, it is important that you look at your beliefs to see if there are any hidden obstacles.

Exercise: Recognizing Beliefs

Find out what you think and believe:

- *What do I think about myself? Do I believe that I am worthy to realize my dreams and achieve something in life?*

- *What do I think about my goals? Do I think they are something I deserve, or do I think I should be satisfied with what I have?*

- *What do I think about the road to get there? Do I have to try hard or can it really be easy?*

Take time for this analysis and write down everything you can think of. It can also be a mixture of "on the one hand" and "on the other hand", through which you recognize that different parts are in conflict with each other.

Our beliefs are shaped by childhood and life experiences and the conclusions we have drawn from them. These have an influence on how we go through life, as the following example shows.

What's Next?

In a workshop one participant said: "Maybe I should be satisfied with what I have. There's always something worse coming!" I was surprised by this statement, because my own conviction is the exact opposite: Something better always follows!

Check for each of these two statements:

What triggers that statement in you?

What do you think of that statement? Do you agree or disagree with it?

Which body perception do you notice when reading this statement?

What is now, after the physical perception, your spontaneous idea? What would you most like to do – or not do?

What results could this produce? What would be possible with that, what wouldn't?

Compare your results to both statements: What is the same and how do they differ?

The thought *"There is always something worse to come"* leads people to fall into a position of carefulness. They change nothing, even if they are dissatisfied or even driven by an inner restlessness and longing for change. They accept their situation and don't manage to change anything – because it could be worse than it already is.

In contrast, I experience people with the basic attitude *"There is always something better to come"* as active and future-oriented. They accept problems as part of life, reflect on events in order to learn from them, and then credit them to the account "experience". This makes it easier for them to let go of negative experiences more quickly and to look to the future with expectation.

Develop Beneficial Thoughts

Whether your thoughts are conducive or limiting for you and your future success is signaled by your body. If you know your limiting beliefs, you can change them and replace them with productive thoughts and thus achieve different results.

Write down any limiting sentences that you notice or that others point out to you. Do not gloss over or censor anything. Just take note of such thoughts. Only if you are honest with yourself can you change the way you talk to yourself – and these are your thoughts first and foremost.

Exercise: Changing Limiting Thoughts

Transform any limiting thought into a supportive sentence that is positive, constructive, and beneficial.

Limiting Thought	*New Statement*
If it were that simple!	*I'll make it easy on myself.*

93

Talk is cheap!	That's a new thought I'm pursuing.
Life's no bed of roses.	Life is the way I make it and wish it to be.
I can't choose my environment.	I accept my environment as it is and make the most of it.
I can't do any of this.	I'm going one step at a time.

If in the future you catch yourself thinking the limiting thought, say to yourself: *Stop! That's not true (anymore)* ... and add to your beneficial sentence: *That's not true anymore. I'll make it easy on myself.* The new statements can serve as personal reinforcement sentences with which you gradually change your inner attitudes and convictions. Another possibility is to turn it into a mantra that you sing to yourself while walking, cooking or cleaning. Until the new sentence has become a matter of fact.

The Root Causes of Blockages Lie Deeper

In addition to the superficial obstacles that are mainly caused by our thoughts, there are also deeper blockages that paralyze our actions. We'd love to act, but we just can't. Something's blocking us. In my experience, many blockages stem from one of the following three areas:

That's What Everybody Does!

There is a popular approach in business life: to look for "best practices", i.e. examples of how others have successfully demonstrated success. This is associated with the conviction that something that has worked once can be transferred to many other situations.

There are also numerous examples of best practice for the achievement of objectives. You get to know them through books, lectures or seminars and try them out. But you can't handle it or fail halfway. Instead of considering yourself incapable, consider this: *What if this path is wrong for you and your project?* With the Encouragement Principle you will find another, namely your own personal way to reach your goal. Here, too, obstacles can appear on the road to success. But with the methods presented in this book, you will find your own way to deal with them.

Help, I Don't Know What I Want!

You have worked on the exercises from the first chapter, but they did little for you. You have no idea what your future might look like and what you really want. Everything you write down feels wrong. The longer you sit before the task, the less clear you can think.

This "I don't know what I want" blockage affects people who have experienced the following situations:

- They were never asked what they wanted. Others have decided for them as a matter of fact – and they have complied.

- It has not been necessary to worry so far. In the past, one thing has joined the other and the results did fit in general.

- They have never learned that their wishes are important. Whenever they showed interest or expressed wishes, they were talked out of it. They followed the ideas of others and thereby lost access to their own desires and dreams.

- They have many different interests and move from one exciting topic to the next. They can't choose any of them. It is difficult for them to stick to a single thing or to choose a goal.

If you find yourself in any of these descriptions and want to change something, pay attention to what attracts your attention at this point in time and what particularly appeals to you. Collect everything that appeals to you. Get support to identify the common thread in your collection or find out how to link multiple interests.

You Can't do That!

And finally, there are those who have ideas, but do not put them on paper or stop at the first concrete steps at the latest. They experience an inner barrier that makes it impossible for them to do anything. They fail to dream of another environment, a new activity or a better relationship because they lack the "permission" to do so.

Manuela, Participant in a Coaching Group for Founders and Business Owners

In the coaching group we experienced Manuela as a woman who was full of ideas. She loved colors and fabrics and was very creative in dealing with them. When it came to creating a business concept from this, she visibly froze. As it turned out, she did not allow herself to earn money with something she perceived as a hobby.

I suggested that she create a personal permit that everyone in the group would sign. No sooner said than done. She framed it and hung it up visibly in her kitchen. This was the first step on her way to a successful and colorful company.

Permission won't come from the outside. As an adult, you can and may decide for yourself whether you want to stay where you are. Or, like Manuela, you can finally give yourself permission to shape your life according to your own wishes.

When Blockages are Deeply Rooted

There are blockages that are so deep that they can hardly be solved with the methods presented in this book. In these cases, it is important to find out the root causes that lie in the family or life history and to resolve them with professional help. Once this has been resolved, you are free enough to discover your own goals and walk the path there with ease.

Dealing Creatively with Obstacles

Usually we try to solve obstacles from the head, or use procedures that we already know. Here you will get to know two possibilities to proceed in a playful way.

Invite Obstacles to Dance

Find a piece of music that you like to move to. The best piece is one that lasts ten minutes or longer. Close your eyes and move to the rhythm of the music for some time until you feel like you're completely connected with yourself. Ask your "ghosts" – the obstacles, resistances and blockages – to show themselves.

- Which ghosts appear before your inner eye and in which form do they appear? What do they look like? What mood are they in? How do they move? What's your own feeling about this?

- Thank everyone for showing up and ask one of them to dance. Say goodbye to the others; they will be picked at a different time.

- Let the obstacle take the lead in this dance. Ask it: *Show me what you want from me and how you can be of use to me.* This will give you a different view of the obstacle or provide insights or surprising aspects.

- Say goodbye to your "dance partner" at the end of that piece of music. Write down what you have learned through this dance.

- If you like, you can gradually dance with the other spirits – right after this one or at another time. Make sure that you are well! This dance should, besides the gain of knowledge, also bring fun.

Elisabeth, Participant in a Coaching Group

My dance with the phlegm, with which I always quarrel, brought an amazing insight. Our movements were barely perceptible, which surprised me at first. When I asked, this information came up: I'll protect you and make sure you move effortlessly.

Talk to Each Other

"Pressure creates counter-pressure" – this sentence already shows that there is no point in resisting or fighting against resistances. Give them a place instead and get to know them better.

Exercise: A Clarifying "Conversation"

Place two chairs opposite each other. Sit on one and place a symbol for your doubt on the other chair. Do not ponder for long, but take any object to represent your doubt. Ask your doubt the following question: What are you trying to tell me?

Then change places and sit in the position of doubt. Take the object in your hand and answer spontaneously.

After the answers change back to the first chair and ask the doubt the next question.

You can also do this exercise in writing and use different colors to mark the position change.

Become and Remain Capable of Acting

Usually it is not so much the inability to deal with fears, doubts and negativity that makes us bother, but the lack of willingness to deal with them. It is so much easier to carry on in the old, familiar way than to deal with obstacles and put them in their place.

This may sound strange to your ears and be contradicted by some. But there's an important question behind it that you need to deal with: Who keeps the hand on the steering wheel and determines the direction? Behind all obstacles are your thoughts, to which you leave the steering wheel instead of putting them in their place. Check yourself out now: *Am I really ready and committed to do everything I can to achieve my goals?*

If you hesitate, put the book aside and wait until you are ready. Stop complaining and enjoy life as it is for now. However, if you decide to achieve your goals and are determined to do everything you can to achieve them, you will find suggestions here on how to deal with fears, doubts and whining fits.

Anxieties

Fears – as well as obstacles – are part of our lives and have a multifaceted function: They drive us to change something. They protect us and warn us of dangers. They brake when we are too fast and show us that there is still something to learn or to clarify. They are an integral part of the achievement of our goals and accompany us constantly. As Susan Jeffers writes in her readable book "Feel the Fear and Do It Anyway", we will never be without fear. It therefore makes sense to deal with them instead of fighting them.

If you accept your fears, you will learn a lot about what they have to say and gain another supporter on your path. Here you will find three options to deal with emerging fears:

Fits the Label?

You have already read about this option. Start with noticing your body sensations and register what you actually feel. Then check whether "fear" is really the right term for this situation.

Stay in Touch!

Feel what you feel without judging or changing any-thing. Stick to this feeling and pay attention to when it changes.

Surprisingly, feelings change when they get attention and are allowed to be present. It is possible that what you have experienced as anxiety before may stop completely after a short time.

What Does Fear Want to Tell You?

Connect with your fear and find out what it wants to tell you. Ask it questions and allow yourself to be surprised by its answers. This is the simple variant.

An alternative is the exercise "A Clarifying Conversation" described above, in which you change positions (see p. 99).

Doubts

If you doubt your intention or your own abilities, you should ask yourself the question: *What does my goal stand for?* There may be a different need behind this than you suspect. Here are some examples of such needs: Recognition from your environment, belonging to a certain group or even the desire to prove something to yourself. Perhaps you associate your project with an attitude towards life that is important to you and which you hope will come about when you have arrived at your destination.

Many people want more ease, freedom or security. In such cases, you should check whether the desired attitude towards life can actually occur through your project or whether it can be achieved by other means.

There are people who basically doubt everything and everyone at first. That's a habit they are often not even aware of. When you realize that this is the case with you, find out what is behind it.

It may be necessary to reexamine individual aspects of your goal and find out whether it is what you really want and whether the motives behind it are still valid.

Whining

Every human being has phases from time to time in which we simply want to moan and feel sorry for ourselves. But how do you prevent yourself from kicking yourself out of the game with it? Very simple: Allow yourself to whine and use a trick for it.

Exercise: Limit the Whining Time!

If you don't get anywhere, question your goal, or keep thinking about what's not working, stop your thought carousel. Say to yourself: Now is not the time!

Take your calendar instead and make an appointment with yourself when you will take time for it – and keep that appointment. Limit the whining time to 15 minutes. Express everything that wears you down, burdens or occupies you – verbally or in writing. Then destroy what you have written down and let it go.

With a limited whining session, you give in to your need and yet remain master of the affairs. This is a clever way to control the inner chaos that precedes a new order and at the same time you care for your soul's well-being.

Easily Around

Before something looks easy, a lot of practice is required – this also applies to the road toward your goal. You have already received many suggestions, some of which are new or unfamiliar. Instead of always moving in the same tracks, try something else. This includes detours as well as the willingness to act despite. Sometimes it will be necessary to be self-confident, even if you feel anything but safe inside.

Contrast It with Something Positive

Brain researchers have discovered that our brain is particularly interested in the happiness hormone dopamine. The more of these we produce, the easier it is for us to try out new things, make wise decisions and pursue our goals. When we worry, fear difficulties or encounter pain, whether imaginary or real, the level of dopamine in the brain drops. The result: we lose interest, motivation and optimism. Such negative thoughts can be countered with regular 60-second bites – a "dopamine dessert", as the neuroscientists Mark Waldman and Dr. Andrew Newberg[3] call it.

Exercise: Dopamine Dessert Prevents Dislike

Stretch and move your arms and legs in a way that gives you maximum pleasure. Stroke with your fingers over the palms of your hands and experience the pleasant feeling that this creates. Stroke your face and scalp. Take a deep breath and enhance the pleasure. Then stroke your hands over your clothes and pay attention to how different the structure of the individual pieces feels.

Breathe through your nose and feel the fresh air coming in through your nostrils. If this feels good, emphasize this feeling

---

[3] Authors of the book "The Power of Compassionate Communication: How Words Can Change Our Lives". Source: Science of Mind, August 2013

when exhaling with the sound "Mmm". Feel this sound vibrate through your body.

Concentrate on the pleasant feeling in your body. Go from on with your attention to all the pleasant smells and noises in your surroundings. Register everything with a "Mmm". Finally, let your eyes wander to all the wonderful colors and shapes that surround you.

During this exercise it is impossible for your brain to think of problems or negatives. In addition, the sound of "Mmm" slows down the thinking process in the frontal lobe of the brain, where negative thoughts arise. This provide your brain with a rest and produces dopamine in the process. After this short break return to your tasks with a feeling of clarity and satisfaction.

Discover Detours

Sometimes we find out that we can't get any further on the usual fairway. Then we need another route. This can look like a detour that takes longer and is further. However, realizing a personal project is not an athletic achievement that depends on reaching the goal as quickly as possible. Obstacles are merely an indication that things are not going any further here or in this way.

First step back a bit. With a little distance, you can see better how big an obstacle is. Perhaps you are already discovering a path that will take you further and try it out. Or you can take the water as a model: it is being guided by the blockage until it can flow freely again. Detours often turn out to be valuable.

Acting Anyway

The title of the aforementioned book by Susan Jeffers "Feel the fear and do it anyway" can serve as a guide for this suggestion: Don't let fears or obstacles stop you from following your own path. Even in difficult situations, there are opportunities to take small steps forward.

Exercise: Getting to "Anyway"

Take three minutes and write down everything you could be doing right now. Stay in the form of possibility: I could... With it you give yourself the freedom and permission to write down even crazy thoughts.

Go through your ideas, choose one spontaneously – and put it into practice right away!

In this way, you will learn that there are always more possibilities than you initially suspect. Through rapid implementation, you will discover that it is possible to remain capable of acting even in challenging situations. This strengthens your self-confidence and brings you step by small step closer to your goal.

Pretend

The role models you discovered in Chapter 3 will help you at this point (see p. 51). How did these people act to achieve their goal self-confidently? What do they do and what do they leave when they experience difficulties? How do they do it? How do you recognize their self-confidence? This provides you with clues for your own approach.

Acquire the skills of your role model. See which ones suit you. Imitate posture, language and procedures. Pretend that you are just as self-confident, assured or successful – even if it is not yet the case. You will quickly notice that it is easier for you to act self-confidently and trustingly every time. With each "acting as if" your inner strength grows and you move more naturally – until it has become a habit.

If Nothing Works at All …

There are moments when nothing works. You are nailed down, have no ideas and know neither off nor on. Instead of blaming yourself, there's only one thing to do: let go of your plans and everything that it attached to it for a moment. Why putting energy into it and wanting to achieve something by force when it leads nowhere?!

Maybe you're asking yourself: *How do I know when to let go?* Important signs are high tension and internal pressure. These signals are provided by your body. If you find that you are trying too hard or that there are a lot of mistakes, say: *Stop! I can't go on like this!* There is no end date to personal goals. That's why nobody pushes you – just yourself. Let go and trust that the solution will soon emerge and that you will continue with new strength. And until then? Here are some suggestions:

Do Something Else

Sometimes materials or information is missing. While you are waiting for it, work on another aspect of your project that is due later. That will keep you flowing. As a side effect, cross-connections, new findings and surprising insights can emerge that serve your project as a whole.

If this is not an alternative, work on a task that has nothing to do with your project. Cleaning, cooking and tidying up are particularly popular and helpful. You are busy with this – an important aspect for many people! A further advantage is that you usually don't think much about these activities and quickly get a sense of achievement. This distracts from the fact that this is not the case with your project right now.

Creative activities such as painting, writing, handicrafts or decorating also occupy the mind and distract from the blockage. The advantage of this: You have to concentrate, deal with something else and often develop "quite incidentally" good ideas for your next steps.

Change Location

Moving to another place – both inside and outside – leads to a change of perspective. While I was writing this book, I withdrew for a week to a holiday home. There I was away from everyday life and could work completely undisturbed. An excursion, a visit to a trade fair, an art exhibition or a visit to the cinema can also lead to inspiration and new inspiration.

Take a Break to Relax

While working intensively on something we easily forget that we also have a body. Only when it gives painful signals do we wake up from our state of highest concentration. Then we need a balance that frees the body from its rigidity. In relaxing the body, the mental tension softens as well and we can continue to work with new momentum.

Find out what's the best way to relax. Here are some suggestions for quick re-energizing:

- a walk in the nature

- dancing or yoga exercises

- stretch and roll like a cat

- a 20-minute break: lie flat and relax your body. A longer sleep break is rather counterproductive here. To avoid falling asleep after all, take a key in your hand. This falls down when you fall asleep and wakes you up before you sink into deep sleep.

- Also use your personal place of power described in chapter 4 (see p. 67).

Next Steps

- Check regularly how easy your steps feel right now. Ask yourself: How could it go easier?

- Use resistance as a clue instead of fighting it. Find out what's behind it and what is its message. Detours provide orientation and show new routes.

- Take a break more often – to clarify, review and align your project.

STAYING IN THE FLOW – SECURING SUCCESS

The approach presented in this book is a personal development process. Instead of the usual expectation "someone has the solution for me" you are challenged to find your own path. Perhaps you have realized that you have everything you need to walk in ease. Which doesn't mean everything's simple and trouble-free. But the tools presented in this book will help you to identify the route that suits you best and to follow it courageously.

At any point along the way, you can decide whether to continue to trust this process, stay curious and have fun. Even if you don't have complete control over individual steps and results, one thing is important: you have most of your experience in your own hands. At every moment you decide with which attitude you look at results or problems: expectant or skeptical, trusting or anxious, calm or always on guard.

This way you influence the design of your route: whether it becomes easy and flowing or whether you experience it as strenuous. With some final thoughts you stay in the flow and secure your further success.

Trust the Process

At the beginning of your journey, despite your ideas and wishes, you do not yet know where you will actually arrive at the end and what you will experience on the way. Over time, more and more details emerge. You learn to live with uncertainty and to focus on what you desire. Two elements support you which – according to the metaphor of the river – work like the embankments that guide the river: your body awareness and trust.

Trust in Yourself and in Life

One part is self-confidence – confidence in yourself, in your abilities and experiences as well as in your desires and dreams from which your goals derive.

This is contrasted with trust in life as such, which is sometimes referred to as "basic trust". Depending on what you experienced in your childhood and youth, this basic trust was strengthened or weakened. And thus, it is easier or harder for you to believe in your own dreams, a self-determined life and a benevolent universe. You are not tied to the past. You can break through old patterns and make new decisions. Sometimes this is not possible by yourself – then you need outside help.

Make it a rule to keep pausing and checking where you stand in this confidence-building process. Connect it with checking your ideas, results and actions and aligning yourself regularly.

Exercise: Pausing Regularly

Put the spotlight on your results and experiences once a week. Make a habit of it, for which you set a fixed date, e.g. Sunday evening.

Check what you had planned and what actually happened during the week:

- *What have you done? What results have been achieved? What experience have you had? Take notes of your achievements in your diary or work book.*

- *What did not work or only partly worked? Let go of what has been finished or what you can't change. Check out where you're still angry – and say goodbye to it. What happened is done and over. Use the suggestions to become non-attached again.*

- *Focus on the week ahead, your next steps and your plans. Set intentions for it.*

Acknowledge Achievements

In spite of regular reviews, we quickly struggle when progress is less than expected, or we lose sight of the small successes. If we do not recognize and appreciate them, our energy level drops and we become discouraged. It helps, however, to regularly acknowledge what has already been achieved – in small as well as in large. This does not take long, is very effective and consists of two parts: Gratitude and appreciation.

Gratitude Increases the Power of Attraction

You may agree right away because you have heard this idea many times before. But do you implement it regularly? Only then will you experience the positive effect.

Most of the time during a day we deal with what *doesn't* work in our lives: We compare ourselves with others and recognize that they are better, more successful and more self-confident. We evaluate everything we see, hear or witness. Very few of it gets positive grades. We also watch news about disasters, disputes or defeats, or see films about murder and other crimes. It takes a lot of energy not to be influenced by this amount of negativity and to keep a positive self-image.

So, make it a habit to be grateful for everything you have in your life. Feel this gratitude and express it. Pay attention to everything that contributes to your progress and appreciate that part of your success – be it your own abilities or the support of others, challenges you have mastered, or agreements you have honored even though you did not feel like it.

Exercise: Pause and Feel

Take a regular break and write it down: I am grateful for ...; I am grateful that ...

Find at least three points each time and notice how it feels. Let this pleasant feeling flow through your body and spread out.

If you pause regularly and consciously and sense your gratitude, you will experience amazing things: You will feel good for long periods of time, your energy level will rise and you will achieve more. Combine this exercise with the next suggestion and multiply the effect.

Appreciation Strengthens Self-Confidence

In addition to gratitude, which is more focused on others, appreciation serves mainly us: for what we do when we are excelling ourselves or stay on track. There are so many things that you can be proud of and appreciate: that you got up this morning instead of staying in bed; that you read this book up to here and tried some exercises out of it immediately; that you helped someone ...

Again, feel this appreciation for yourself. Maybe it will be difficult for you at first. Then your bar is too high. Start with the obvious. Then move on to little things that you have found difficult and which you have nevertheless done. As time goes by, larger steps are taken and your self-esteem increases more and more – especially if you do the following exercise in writing.

Exercise: Keeping an Appreciation Diary

Take a small notebook in DIN-A6 / 4x6 inches format. Fill one page every day by adding to the initial sentence: I value myself for ... / I value that ... *(choose what feels easier to add to)*

Don't stop until the page is full. Do this task for 30 days and you will see your self-confidence grow.

Pause several times a day and combine gratitude and appreciation, e.g. before starting a new task, before lunch, in the evening before you go to bed. Set the alarm function on your phone to remind you every three hours. Choose a rhythm that suits your daily routine.

Find three points for which you are grateful and three aspects for what you value, feel good about or are proud of. Make sure that you do not stay in your head, but feel it. With a little practice, it takes one minute at most and is a short, very effective break in your daily activities.

Continue to Expand Successes

For most people, staying on track is the hardest part. After the first euphoria and enthusiasm for your project, you quickly return to everyday life and your duties. Especially when, after the first successes, steps need to be taken that require more courage and commitment. Then the decision is made as to who belongs to the "hang-ons" and who sinks back into the mass of "dispatchers". It's in your hand. With the Encouragement Principle, you will find your own personal path that is as unique as your fingerprint. The following recommendations will help you:

Stay Relaxed

"If things don't go the way you want them to, imagine something else," recommends a Polynesian proverb. It works better if you accept that not everything is up to you. Instead of whining about it and running up against it, relax. You can't usually do anything about it anyway. Stay open and curious about everything else that happens when you are "just" present. Don't do anything, just stay with what's going on. Perceive, hold the energy and wait. This is a big challenge for many people.

Create Habits

Habits are created by doing things regularly. Repeat daily all the steps you have chosen to do. Take ad-vantage of the key questions, which are summarized once again at the end of this book. At first somewhat bumpy and unfamiliar steps are slowly transformed into a beaten path that develops into a motorway over time. To integrate new habits, you usually need some stamina. This will be acquired easier when you realize that you are slowly approaching your goal and that you experience a sense of achievement.

Here are a few recommendations to develop habits for your goal:

- Start the day with your project. Put a short version of it in a place where you can see it automatically every morning, e.g. on the bedside table or at your place at the breakfast table.

- The morning would also be a good time for the daily ritual. Alternatively, schedule it after dinner before starting other activities. Here, too, it is helpful to install a reminder anchor, e.g. place your diary or work book there.

- Throughout the day, set yourself an alarm clock with a small memo: *Pause and attention to my body.*

- Enter a fixed date for weekly planning in your calendar. This includes review, advance planning and work steps.

- Enjoy your path and the individual steps. Try out what suits best for you, your daily routine and your project.

Enlarge the Tub

After she had realized her first big project, a colleague said this apt sentence: *Each realized goal entails further ones.* Prepare yourself mentally for additional projects beyond the one you focused on in the course of this book. Pay attention to what you encounter on your route right and left and collect these ideas. You never know what they are good for and when you need them. Collect everything that attracts your attention.

Perhaps your next project will emerge from this collection, or perhaps it will be something else. In any case, you will sharpen your perception of opportunities and potentials. Fill your tub of possibilities with these ideas. Thus, you will stick less to the one project you chose at the beginning. You become freer in your decision when it turns out that something else is more important. There are so many options that are also worthwhile to be realized easily and courageously. Not because you have no other choice, but because you have chosen it with all your heart.

Outlook

Use – one after the other – the strategies and procedures offered in this book. Start out with curiosity and try out variations. The elements of the Encouraging Principle serve as a guideline for this.

Make your own experiences: *Find your path – and walk it courageously!* You will experience what many people have experienced before: an increase in joy of living, satisfaction and energy. I wish you all the best for your journey!

ABOUT THE AUTHOR

For more than 25 years, Ulrike Bergmann has been encouraging founders, small business owners and people undergoing professional change to achieve their personal goals and realize their entrepreneurial dreams.

As a coach, consultant and small business owner herself she supports her clients to take their desires and ideas seriously and shows them how to actively shape their lives and their businesses according to their wishes, recognize their own path and walk it courageously and easily.

She is the author of four successful guidebooks and regularly offers expert knowledge, tools and suggestions in her blog. In German-speaking countries she became well-known through the introduction of and her work with success teams and other forms of support teams.

Today she sees it as her mission to teach women to recognize their self-efficacy and to encourage them to use it powerfully for the greater good of all people.

Further information about her work and offerings can be found at www.die-mutmacherin.de.